30Minute
Recipes

Strawberry Cheesecake Trifle (p. 99)

Ladle Out Homemade Comfort...In Minutes!

IN TODAY'S world, busy cooks appreciate family-pleasing dishes that come together in a snap. That's why we've compiled this collection of 223 no-fuss recipes...each of which is table-ready in just half an hour or less!

As you browse through the *Best of Country 30-Minute Recipes*, you'll notice that most of the scrumptious submissions come from on-the-go cooks. Their time in the kitchen is limited, but they still want to feed their families down-home foods loaded with flavor.

In this book, you'll find the made-in-minutes main courses, speedy side dishes and super-quick snacks these folks use to beat the clock. With their tried-and-true favorites at your fingertips, whipping up a home-style delight is easier than ever.

Best of Country 30-Minute Recipes is the answer to your dinnertime dilemmas, whether you need beefy main courses or chicken suppers that are ready in a pinch. You'll also find chapters devoted to effortless pork and seafood entrees, as well as a section of complete menus you can bring to the table in a half hour (see p. 88).

Dinner accompaniments are a breeze with the savory sensations found in "Streamlined Side Dishes" (p. 34); or consider the refreshing ideas offered in "Swift Soups, Salads & Sandwiches" (p. 24).

Need a quick nibble or a last-minute classroom treat? Turn to page 14 for dozens of simple snacks. Similarly, page 96 lists more than 20 delicious desserts that tickle the sweet tooth without taxing your time.

In addition to fast breakfast fare and easy appetizers, other great timesavers include tips to speed up prep work and indexes highlighting recipes that take only 15 minutes to prepare.

Whether you're looking for an entree that's ready in moments or a no-fuss sweet to share with friends, the *Best of Country 30-Minute Recipes* is one kitchen tool you'll be sure to reach for time and again.

Enjoy an Instant Dinner Tonight

We know the value of meal-in-one dishes such as casseroles and stir-fries, so we marked those recipes with the icon at left. You'll also find a listing of these 67 recipes in the index starting on page 106.

Senior Editor/Books: Mark Hagen
Art Director: Gretchen Trautman
Vice President/Books: Heidi Reuter Lloyd
Layout Designer: Kathy Crawford
Associate Layout Designer: Julie Stone
Proofreader: Linne Bruskewitz
Editorial Assistant: Barb Czysz
Associate Food Editors: Coleen Martin, Diane Werner
Assistant Food Editor: Karen Scales
Senior Recipe Editor: Sue A. Jurack
Recipe Editors: Mary King, Christine Rukavena
Food Photographers: Rob Hagen, Dan Roberts, Jim Wieland
Associate Photographer: Lori Foy
Food Stylist: Sara Thompson
Set Stylists: Jennifer Bradley Vent, Stephanie Marchese
Assistant Set Stylist: Melissa Haberman
Photo Studio Coordinator: Suzanne Kern

Creative Director: Ardyth Cope
Senior Vice President/Editor in Chief: Catherine Cassidy
President: Barbara Newton
Founder: Roy Reiman

©2007 Reiman Media Group, Inc.
5400 S. 60th St., Greendale WI 53129

International Standard Book Number (10): 0-89821-542-0
International Standard Book Number (13): 978-0-89821-542-7
Library of Congress Control Number: 2006931744
All rights reserved.
Printed in U.S.A.

Pictured on front cover: Crab-Stuffed Chicken (p. 64), Sweet Sesame Salad (p. 32) and Pineapple Orange Cheesecake (p. 100).
Pictured on back cover: Gingered Pork Tenderloin (p. 76).

Home-Style Country Sausage (p. 10)
Very Veggie Omelet (p. 9)

Chapter 1

Brisk Breakfasts

You don't have to scramble around the kitchen at the crack of dawn to enjoy a hearty, homemade breakfast. The eye-openers in this chapter come together in moments!

Chicken and Egg Hash

(Pictured below)
Prep/Total Time: 30 min.

Joyce Price • Whitefish, Ontario
This recipe is one of my daughter's favorites. To reduce cooking time and clean out the fridge, dice up leftover potatoes and chicken for this dish.

      4 bacon strips, diced
      1 medium onion, chopped
      2 garlic cloves, minced
      1 pound boneless skinless chicken breasts, cubed
      2 large potatoes, peeled and diced
      1 tablespoon vegetable oil
  1/2 cup frozen peas, thawed
  1/2 cup frozen corn, thawed
      2 tablespoons minced fresh parsley
  3/4 teaspoon salt
  1/8 teaspoon pepper
      4 eggs

In a large skillet, cook bacon until crisp. Remove with a slotted spoon to paper towels to drain. In the drippings, saute onion and garlic until tender. Stir in the chicken, potatoes and oil. Cover and cook for 10 minutes or until the potatoes and chicken are tender, stirring once. Stir in peas, corn, parsley, salt and pepper.

   Make four wells in the hash; break an egg into each well. Cover and cook over low heat for 8-10 minutes or until eggs are completely set. Sprinkle with bacon. **Yield:** 4 servings.

Chicken and Egg Hash

Sweet Ham Steak

Prep/Total Time: 15 min.

Nancy Smits • Markesan, Wisconsin
You need just two items to sweetly season this ham steak. It's a quick and easy addition to any meal.

      1 bone-in fully cooked ham steak (2 pounds)
      5 tablespoons butter, cubed
      5 tablespoons brown sugar

In a large skillet over medium heat, brown ham steak on both sides; drain. Remove ham.

   In the same skillet, melt the butter; stir in brown sugar. Return ham to skillet; cook until heated through, turning often. **Yield:** 6-8 servings.

Bacon Cheddar Quiche

Prep/Total Time: 20 min.

Val Forsythe • Albert Lea, Minnesota
Whenever company stays overnight, I make this microwave breakfast. It only takes about 20 minutes from start to finish.

   14 bacon strips, cooked and crumbled
      1 cup (4 ounces) shredded cheddar cheese
      1 jar (6 ounces) sliced mushrooms, drained
      1 tablespoon dried minced onion
      5 eggs
      1 can (5 ounces) evaporated milk
  1/4 teaspoon cayenne pepper

In a greased 9-in. microwave-safe pie plate, layer the bacon, cheese, mushrooms and onion. In a large bowl, beat the eggs, milk and cayenne; pour over the onion.

   Microwave, uncovered, on high for 6 minutes, stirring twice. Cook 2-3 minutes longer or until a knife inserted near the center comes out clean. Let stand for 5 minutes or until set. Cut into wedges. **Yield:** 4-6 servings.

Editor's Note: This recipe was tested with an 850-watt microwave.

Quick TIP Don't have time in the morning to thaw frozen juice concentrate? Set the concentrate in a blender with a few teaspoons of water. Then process it for a moment or two.

Strawberry-Topped Waffles

Strawberry-Topped Waffles
(Pictured above)
Prep/Total Time: 30 min.

Sue Mackey • Galesburg, Illinois
Topped with a sweet strawberry sauce, these tender, from-scratch waffles will make your next breakfast or brunch truly special.

>   2 pints fresh strawberries
>   5 tablespoons sugar, *divided*
>   2 cups all-purpose flour
>   2 teaspoons baking powder
>   1/2 teaspoon baking soda
>   1/2 teaspoon salt
>   2 eggs
>   2 cups (16 ounces) sour cream
>   1 cup milk
>   3 tablespoons vegetable oil
> Whipped topping *or* vanilla ice cream
> Additional strawberries, optional

Place strawberries and 3 tablespoons of sugar in a food processor or blender. Cover and process until coarsely chopped; set aside.

In a large bowl, combine the flour, baking powder, baking soda, salt and remaining sugar. In another bowl, combine the eggs, sour cream, milk and oil; stir into dry ingredients just until combined.

Preheat waffle iron. Fill and bake according to manufacturer's directions. Serve with strawberry topping, whipped topping and additional strawberries if desired. **Yield:** 6-8 waffles.

Mini Coffee Cakes
(Pictured below)
Prep/Total Time: 30 min.

Dena Engelland • Sterling, Kansas
These moist, buttery muffins that feature a nutty topping are so easy to prepare. Stir up a batch of the cute cakes and let them bake alongside your main course while you fix the morning coffee, stir the orange juice and set the breakfast table.

>   1/3 cup butter, softened
>   1/4 cup sugar
>   1 egg
> 1-1/2 cups all-purpose flour
>   1 package (3.4 ounces) instant vanilla
>   pudding mix
>   1 tablespoon baking powder
>   1/4 teaspoon salt
> 1-1/4 cups milk
>   1/2 cup chopped walnuts

TOPPING:
>   1/2 cup chopped walnuts
>   1/3 cup packed brown sugar
>   2 tablespoons butter, melted
>   1/4 teaspoon ground cinnamon

In a large mixing bowl, cream butter and sugar. Beat in egg. Combine flour, pudding mix, baking powder and salt; add to the creamed mixture alternately with milk. Beat until blended. Stir in walnuts.

Fill paper-lined muffin cups two-thirds full. Combine topping ingredients; sprinkle over batter. Bake at 375° for 20-25 minutes or until a toothpick inserted near the center comes out clean. Cool for 10 minutes; remove from pan to a wire rack. **Yield:** about 1 dozen.

Mini Coffee Cakes

Lightly Scrambled Eggs

Lightly Scrambled Eggs
(Pictured above)
Prep/Total Time: 15 min.

Patricia Kaliska • Phillips, Wisconsin
Wake up your taste buds with this fluffy main course, featuring sour cream, green onions and cheese.

>   9 egg whites
>   3 eggs
> 1/2 cup reduced-fat sour cream
> 1/4 cup fat-free milk
>   2 green onions, thinly sliced
> 1/4 teaspoon salt
> 1/8 teaspoon pepper
>   6 drops yellow food coloring, optional
> 3/4 cup shredded reduced-fat cheddar cheese

In a large bowl, whisk the egg whites and eggs. Add the sour cream, milk, onions, salt, pepper and food coloring if desired. Pour into a large nonstick skillet coated with nonstick cooking spray. Cook and gently stir over medium heat until eggs are completely set. Remove from the heat. Sprinkle with cheese; cover and let stand for 5 minutes or until cheese is melted. **Yield:** 6 servings.

Glazed Bacon
Prep/Total Time: 30 min.

Janet Nolan • Navesink, New Jersey
Everyone agrees that this bacon is just as sweet as candy due to its brown sugar and orange juice glaze. My mom made it for special-occasion breakfasts, now I serve it often at my home.

>   1 pound sliced bacon
>   1 cup packed brown sugar
> 1/4 cup orange juice
>   2 tablespoons Dijon mustard

Place bacon on a rack in an ungreased 15-in. x 10-in. x 1-in. baking pan. Bake at 350° for 10 minutes; drain. Combine the brown sugar, orange juice and mustard; pour half over bacon. Bake for 10 minutes. Turn bacon and drizzle with remaining glaze. Bake 15 minutes longer or until golden brown. Place bacon on waxed paper until set. Serve warm. **Yield:** 8 servings.

Apple Ham Hotcakes
(Pictured below)
Prep/Total Time: 30 min.

Kelly Williams • La Porte, Indiana
Hearty ham, sweet applesauce and a hint of caraway flavor these fast buttermilk pancakes. They're so delicious, I often serve them hot off the griddle without syrup.

>   1 cup all-purpose flour
>   1 tablespoon baking powder
>   1 tablespoon brown sugar
> 1/2 teaspoon baking soda
> 1/2 teaspoon salt
> 1/2 teaspoon caraway seeds, crushed, optional
>   1 egg
>   1 cup buttermilk
> 3/4 cup chunky applesauce
>   2 tablespoons butter, melted
> 3/4 cup cubed fully cooked ham
> Warm maple syrup, optional

In a large bowl, combine the first five ingredients and caraway seeds if desired. In a small bowl, beat the egg, buttermilk, applesauce, and butter; stir into dry ingredients just until moistened. Fold in ham.

Pour batter by 1/4 cupfuls onto a lightly greased hot griddle; turn when bubbles form on top of pancakes. Cook until second side is golden brown. Serve with syrup if desired. **Yield:** 15 pancakes.

Apple Ham Hotcakes

Croissant French Toast

Very Veggie Omelet
(Pictured on page 4)
Prep/Total Time: 20 min.

Jan Houberg • Reddick, Illinois
I enjoy preparing this filling omelet for my husband, who appreciates new breakfasts. It's chock-full of garden goodness and a snap to prepare.

    1   small onion, chopped
  1/4   cup chopped green pepper
    1   tablespoon butter
    1   small zucchini, chopped
  3/4   cup chopped tomato
  1/4   teaspoon dried oregano
  1/8   teaspoon pepper
    4   egg whites
  1/4   cup water
  1/4   teaspoon cream of tartar
  1/4   teaspoon salt
  1/4   cup egg substitute
  1/2   cup shredded reduced-fat cheddar cheese,
        divided

In a large nonstick skillet, saute onion and green pepper in butter until tender. Add the zucchini, tomato, oregano and pepper. Cook and stir for 5-8 minutes or until vegetables are tender and liquid is nearly evaporated. Set aside and keep warm.

In a mixing bowl, beat egg whites, water, cream of tartar and salt until stiff peaks form. Place egg substitute in another bowl; fold in egg white mixture. Pour into a 10-in. ovenproof skillet coated with nonstick cooking spray. Cook over medium heat for 5 minutes or until bottom is lightly browned.

Bake at 350° for 9-10 minutes or until a knife inserted near the center comes out clean. Spoon vegetable mixture over one side; sprinkle with half of the cheese. To fold, score middle of omelet with a sharp knife; fold omelet over filling. Transfer to a warm platter. Sprinkle with remaining cheese. Cut in half to serve. **Yield:** 2 servings.

Croissant French Toast
(Pictured at left)
Prep/Total Time: 30 min.

June Dickerson • Philippi, West Virginia
More like a scrumptious dessert than a main dish, this rich French toast is topped with two sauces...one of which includes ice cream. I cut the croissants into shapes with a cookie cutter for my young grandson. He even asks for the "ice cream sauce" on pancakes!

  1/2   cup sugar
    1   tablespoon all-purpose flour
    2   cups heavy whipping cream
    4   egg yolks
    1   tablespoon vanilla extract
    2   scoops vanilla ice cream
BERRY SAUCE:
    2   scoops vanilla ice cream
    2   cups fresh raspberries *or* frozen
        unsweetened raspberries
    2   tablespoons sugar
FRENCH TOAST:
    3   eggs
    4   croissants, split
    2   tablespoons butter

In a large saucepan, combine the sugar and flour. Stir in cream until smooth. Cook and stir over medium-high heat until thickened and bubbly. Reduce heat; cook and stir 2 minutes longer. Remove from the heat. Stir a small amount of hot filling into egg yolks; return all to the pan, stirring constantly. Cook and stir until mixture reaches 160°.

Remove from the heat. Gently stir in vanilla and ice cream until the ice cream is melted. Place plastic wrap over the surface of the sauce; cool.

For berry sauce, combine raspberries and sugar in a saucepan. Simmer, uncovered, for 2-3 minutes. Remove from the heat; set aside.

In a shallow bowl, beat eggs. Dip both sides of croissants in egg mixture. On a griddle, brown croissants on both sides in butter. Serve with vanilla and berry sauces. **Yield:** 4 servings.

Quick TIP
Frying bacon can be messy. Save time by frying several strips at once. Put the extra strips on a baking sheet, cover it with foil and set it in the freezer. Once frozen, store the strips in a resealable bag in the freezer. You can reheat as many as needed on busy mornings.

BLT Egg Bake

BLT Egg Bake
(Pictured above)
Prep/Total Time: 30 min.

1 DISH MEAL

Priscilla Detrick • Catoosa, Oklahoma
One of our favorites is a BLT sandwich, so I created this recipe to combine those flavors in a "dressier" dish. It was such a hit, I served it to my church group at a brunch I hosted. I received lots of compliments and wrote out the recipe many times.

- 1/4 cup mayonnaise
- 5 slices bread, toasted
- 4 slices process American cheese
- 12 bacon strips, cooked and crumbled
- 4 eggs
- 1 medium tomato, halved and sliced
- 2 tablespoons butter
- 2 tablespoons all-purpose flour
- 1/4 teaspoon salt
- 1/8 teaspoon pepper
- 1 cup milk
- 1/2 cup shredded cheddar cheese
- 2 green onions, thinly sliced

Shredded lettuce

Spread mayonnaise on one side of each slice of toast and cut into small pieces. Arrange toast, mayonnaise side up, in a greased 8-in. square baking dish. Top with cheese slices and bacon.

In a large skillet, fry eggs over medium heat until completely set; place over bacon. Top with tomato slices; set aside.

In a small saucepan, melt butter. Stir in flour, salt and pepper until smooth. Gradually add milk. Bring to a boil; cook and stir for 2 minutes or until thickened. Pour over tomato. Sprinkle with cheddar cheese and onions. Bake, uncovered, at 325° for 10 minutes. Cut in squares; serve with lettuce. **Yield:** 4 servings.

Home-Style Country Sausage
(Pictured on page 4)
Prep/Total Time: 20 min.

Linda Murray • Allenstown, New Hampshire
My family loves breakfast sausage, but I wanted to reduce the fat and calories in the side dish without increasing my time in the kitchen. This version, which uses ground turkey, is nicely spiced with garlic, sage, allspice, thyme and cayenne pepper.

- 1 medium tart apple, peeled and shredded
- 1/2 cup cooked brown rice
- 2 tablespoons grated onion
- 2 garlic cloves, minced
- 1-1/2 teaspoons rubbed sage
- 1 teaspoon salt
- 1/2 teaspoon pepper
- 1/2 teaspoon dried thyme
- 1/8 teaspoon cayenne pepper
- 1/8 teaspoon ground allspice
- 1 pound lean ground turkey

In a large bowl, combine the first 10 ingredients. Crumble turkey over mixture and mix well. Shape into eight 1/2-in. thick patties.

In a large nonstick skillet coated with nonstick cooking spray, cook patties for 4-6 minutes on each side or until juices run clear. **Yield:** 8 patties.

Cream-Topped Grapes
Prep/Total Time: 15 min.

Vioda Geyer • Uhrichsville, Ohio
I dress up bunches of red and green grapes with a decadent dressing that comes together in moments. Dollop the heavenly, four-ingredient sauce over your favorite combination of fruit.

- 4 ounces cream cheese, softened
- 1/4 cup sugar
- 1/2 teaspoon vanilla extract
- 1/2 cup sour cream
- 3 cups seedless green grapes
- 3 cups seedless red grapes

In a small mixing bowl, beat the cream cheese, sugar and vanilla. Add the sour cream; mix well. Divide grapes among individual serving bowls; dollop with topping. **Yield:** 8 servings.

Mixed Fruit Cup
Prep/Total Time: 5 min.

Florine Bruns • Fredericksburg, Texas
Two cans of fruit and a little whipped cream are all you need for a sweet start to the day.

Cornmeal Waffle Sandwiches

ing to manufacturer's directions until golden brown. Spread mayonnaise on six waffles; top each with bacon, tomato, salt, pepper and remaining waffles. Serve immediately. **Yield:** 6 servings.

Orange Raisin Muffins

(Pictured below)
Prep/Total Time: 30 min.

Robert Taylor • Mesa, Arizona
Lots of oranges and raisins are grown in our state, and we think this is the perfect treat to showcase them.

   1 medium navel orange
1/2 cup orange juice
1/2 cup butter, melted
   1 egg
1-1/2 cups all-purpose flour
3/4 cup sugar
   1 teaspoon baking powder
   1 teaspoon baking soda
   1 teaspoon salt
1/2 cup raisins

Peel orange; place peel in a blender or food processor. Separate orange into segments; place in blender. Add orange juice; cover and process until well blended. Add butter and egg.

In a large bowl, combine the flour, sugar, baking powder, baking soda and salt. Stir in orange mixture just until moistened. Fold in raisins.

Fill greased or paper-line muffin cup two-thirds full. Bake at 400° for 15-20 minutes or until a toothpick comes out clean. Cool for 5 minutes before removing from pan to a wire rack. **Yield:** 1 dozen.

   1 can (15-1/4 ounces) sliced peaches,
     drained
   1 can (15 ounces) fruit cocktail, drained
Whipped cream

Spoon peaches and fruit cocktail into individual dishes. Top with whipped cream. **Yield:** 4 servings.

Cornmeal Waffle Sandwiches

(Pictured above)
Prep/Total Time: 30 min.

Stacy Joura • Stoneboro, Pennsylvania
Craving a sandwich for breakfast? Try this deliciously different idea that features crisp bacon and fresh tomatoes between two homemade, cornmeal waffles. Prepare the waffles ahead of time, reheating them in the toaster for quick assembly.

3/4 cup all-purpose flour
3/4 cup cornmeal
   1 tablespoon baking powder
   1 tablespoon sugar
   1 teaspoon salt
   2 eggs, *separated*
   1 cup milk
   3 tablespoons butter, melted
1/2 cup shredded cheddar cheese
Mayonnaise
 12 bacon strips, cooked and drained
   2 small tomatoes, sliced
Salt and pepper to taste

In a large mixing bowl, combine the first five ingredients. In another bowl, beat egg yolks. Add milk and butter; stir into dry ingredients just until moistened. Stir in cheese.

In a small mixing bowl, beat egg whites until stiff peaks form; fold into the batter.

Bake 12 waffles in a preheated waffle iron accord-

Orange Raisin Muffins

Breakfast Pizza

Breakfast Pizza
(Pictured above)
Prep/Total Time: 30 min.

Christy Hinrichs • Parkville, Missouri
Eggs and hash browns have extra pizzazz when they're served up on a pizza pan. My family requests this fun breakfast often, and it's a snap to make with a prebaked crust. I adjust the "heat index" of the toppings to suit the taste buds of my guests.

> 2 cups frozen shredded hash brown potatoes
> 1/4 teaspoon ground cumin
> 1/4 teaspoon chili powder
> 2 tablespoons canola oil, *divided*
> 1 cup egg substitute
> 2 tablespoons fat-free milk
> 1/4 teaspoon salt
> 2 green onions, chopped
> 2 tablespoons diced sweet red pepper
> 1 tablespoon finely chopped jalapeno pepper
> 1 garlic clove, minced
> 1 prebaked Italian bread shell crust (16 ounces)
> 1/2 cup salsa
> 3/4 cup shredded cheddar cheese

In a nonstick skillet, cook hash browns, cumin and chili powder in 1 tablespoon oil over medium heat until golden. Remove and keep warm. In a bowl, beat egg substitute, milk and salt; set aside. In the same skillet, saute the onions, peppers and garlic in remaining oil until tender. Add egg mixture. Cook and stir over medium heat until almost set. Remove from the heat.

Place crust on an ungreased 14-in. pizza pan. Spread salsa over crust. Top with egg mixture. Sprinkle with hash browns and cheese. Bake at 375° for 8-10 minutes or until cheese is melted. **Yield:** 6 slices.

Editor's Note: When cutting or seeding hot peppers, use rubber or plastic gloves to protect your hands. Avoid touching your face.

Honeydew Kiwi Cooler
Prep/Total Time: 5 min.

The Taste of Home Test Kitchen staff suggests you make a big pitcher of this thick, fruity beverage because your family members are sure to ask for seconds! The quick quencher has a refreshing melon flavor and gets its creamy consistency from fat-free yogurt.

> 3 cups cubed honeydew
> 2 kiwifruit, peeled and cubed
> 1/2 cup fat-free plain yogurt
> 2 tablespoons honey
> 1 cup ice cubes
> 2 to 3 drops green food coloring, optional

In a blender, combine all ingredients; cover and process until blended. Pour into chilled glasses; serve immediately. **Yield:** 4 servings.

Banana Bran Muffins
Prep/Total Time: 25 min.

Shelley Mitchell • Baldur, Manitoba
Our four daughters love to bake and eat these simple spiced muffins. With a little help from myself and my mom, the girls are all learning to be great bakers.

> 1-1/2 cups all-purpose flour
> 1 cup oat bran
> 1/2 cup whole wheat flour
> 1 tablespoon ground cinnamon
> 2 teaspoons baking powder
> 2 teaspoons baking soda
> 1/2 teaspoon ground nutmeg
> 1/4 teaspoon allspice
> 2 eggs
> 1 cup orange juice
> 1/2 cup sugar
> 1/2 cup packed brown sugar
> 1/2 cup vegetable oil
> 1 cup mashed ripe bananas (2 to 3 medium)
> 1/2 cup chopped walnuts

In a large bowl, combine the first eight ingredients. In another bowl, beat the eggs, juice, sugars and oil. Stir into dry ingredients just until moistened. Fold in bananas and nuts.

Fill greased or paper-lined muffin cups two-thirds full. Bake at 400° for 15-18 minutes or until a toothpick comes out clean. Cool for 5 minutes before removing from pans to wire racks. Serve warm. **Yield:** 2 dozen.

Flavorful Frittata
Prep/Total Time: 30 min.

Annette Self • Junction City, Ohio
Slices of this no-stress frittata make a wonderful start to any day. Loaded with mushrooms, pork sausage and cheese, the basil-seasoned egg dish is surprisingly topped with a little spaghetti sauce.

      1 small onion, chopped
      1 jar (4-1/2 ounces) sliced mushrooms, drained
      1 cup cooked bulk pork sausage
      1 to 2 tablespoons vegetable oil
    12 eggs
  1/4 cup half-and-half cream
      1 teaspoon dried basil
  1/2 teaspoon salt
      1 cup (4 ounces) shredded part-skim mozzarella cheese
      2 cups meatless spaghetti sauce, warmed

In a large nonstick skillet, saute the onion, mushrooms and sausage in oil until onion is tender. Meanwhile, in a mixing bowl, beat eggs, cream, basil and salt; pour over sausage mixture.

As eggs set, lift edges, allowing uncooked portion to flow underneath. When eggs are nearly set, sprinkle with cheese. Cook until the cheese is melted. Cut into wedges; serve with spaghetti sauce. **Yield:** 8 servings.

Yogurt Breakfast Drink
Prep/Total Time: 5 min.

Renee Gastineau • Seattle, Washington
I bet your sleepy heads will savor this light and dreamy smoothie. Simply blend yogurt, milk and orange juice concentrate for a fresh start to any morning.

      2 cups (16 ounces) reduced-fat vanilla yogurt
      2 cups (16 ounces) reduced-fat peach yogurt
  1/2 cup frozen orange juice concentrate
  1/2 cup fat-free milk
      2 cups ice cubes

In a blender or food processor, combine the first four ingredients; cover and process until smooth. Add ice cubes; cover and process until smooth. Pour into glasses; serve immediately. **Yield:** 6 servings.

Fruit Pancake Roll-Ups
Prep/Total Time: 15 min.

Wendy Moylan • Crystal Lake, Illinois
A few moments are all you need for this treat. Sweetened sour cream and fruit pie filling add flavor and richness to leftover pancakes. They're tasty for brunch...or dessert.

  1/4 cup sour cream
  1/2 teaspoon confectioners' sugar
      4 large pancakes, warmed
  1/2 cup strawberry *or* raspberry pie filling
Fresh fruit and additional pie filling, optional

In a large bowl, combine the sour cream and sugar. Spread over warm pancakes; top with pie filling. Roll up jelly-roll style. Serve with fruit and additional pie filling if desired. **Yield:** 4 servings.

Brunch Scramble
(Pictured below)
Prep/Total Time: 30 min.

Valerie Putsey • Winamac, Indiana
When I have overnight guests, I serve this speedy skillet dish for breakfast. Onion, green pepper and mushrooms add a bounty of flavor folks love.

      1 medium red onion, chopped
      1 medium green pepper, chopped
      1 jar (4-1/2 ounces) sliced mushrooms, drained
      3 tablespoons butter
    12 eggs
  3/4 cup half-and-half cream
  1-1/2 teaspoons salt
  1/4 teaspoon pepper
  1-1/2 cups (6 ounces) shredded cheddar cheese
      1 tablespoon minced chives

In a large skillet, saute the onion, green pepper and mushrooms in butter until crisp-tender.

Meanwhile, in a large mixing bowl, beat the eggs, cream, salt and pepper; add to skillet. Cook over medium heat until eggs are almost set, stirring occasionally. Sprinkle with cheese and chives. Cover and cook until eggs are completely set and cheese is melted. **Yield:** 6 servings.

Brunch Scramble

Cheesy Zucchini Bites (p. 23)

Speedy Snacks &
Easy Appetizers

There's always time for a late-night bite, after-school nibble or between-meal snack...particularly with the no-fuss munchies and minute-saving treats found here!

Chili Artichoke Dip

(pictured below)
Prep/Total Time: 25 min.

Leanne Mueller • Stockton, California
It's not tricky to prepare this warm and tempting dip. It's cheesy and tasty with a bit of zip from the chilies and marinated artichokes.

>   1 can (14 ounces) water-packed artichoke
>   hearts, rinsed, drained and chopped
>   1 jar (6-1/2 ounces) marinated artichoke
>   hearts, drained and chopped
>   1 can (4 ounces) chopped green chilies
>   3 cups (12 ounces) shredded cheddar cheese
>   1/4 cup mayonnaise
> Assorted crackers *or* tortilla chips

In a bowl, combine the artichokes, chilies, cheese and mayonnaise. Transfer to a greased 8-in. square baking dish. Bake, uncovered, at 350° for 20-25 minutes or until cheese is melted. Serve warm with crackers or tortilla chips. **Yield:** about 3-1/2 cups.

Editor's Note: Reduced-fat or fat-free mayonnaise may not be substituted for regular mayonnaise in this recipe.

Chili Artichoke Dip

Ham and Swiss Snacks

Prep/Total Time: 25 min.

Beth Gambro • Yorkville, Illinois
Following a ball game or for a fun after-school treat, ravenous teenagers can prepare this satisfying snack in a jiffy. It's an easy combination of ham, cheese and apples on a no-fuss crust.

>   2 tubes (8 ounces *each*) refrigerated crescent
>   rolls
>   2 tablespoons prepared mustard
>   2 tablespoons dried parsley flakes
>   2 tablespoons finely chopped onion
>   1 tablespoon butter, softened
>   1 cup chopped peeled tart apple
>   1 cup chopped fully cooked ham
>   3/4 cups shredded Swiss cheese
>   2 tablespoons grated Parmesan cheese

Unroll crescent dough; pat onto the bottom and up the sides of an ungreased 15-in. x 10-in. x 1-in. baking pan. Seal seams and perforations. Bake at 375° for 10-12 minutes or until lightly browned.

Combine mustard, parsley, onion and butter; spread over crust. Sprinkle with apple, ham and cheeses. Bake 5-10 minutes longer or until cheese is melted. Cut into squares. **Yield:** 2 dozen.

Cheery Tomato Bites

Prep/Total Time: 30 min.

David Bostedt • Zephyrhills, Florida
Green onions and crumbled bacon make a savory filling in these colorful tomatoes. They seem like a lot of work but come together very easily.

>   2 pints cherry tomatoes
>   1 package (8 ounces) cream cheese, softened
>   6 bacon strips, cooked and crumbled
>   1/4 cup minced green onions
>   1/4 cup minced fresh parsley
>   1/4 teaspoon Worcestershire sauce

Cut a thin slice of the top of each tomato. Scoop out and discard pulp. Invert the tomatoes on a paper towel to drain. Meanwhile, combine remaining ingredients in a small bowl; mix well. Spoon into tomatoes. Refrigerate until serving. **Yield:** about 4 dozen.

Calico Cheese Dip

Sesame Chicken Bites
(pictured below)
Prep/Total Time: 30 min.

Kathy Green • Layton, New Jersey
So tender and tasty, these chicken appetizers are enhanced by a honey-mustard dipping sauce. I used to prepare several hors d'oeuvres for our holiday open house, and these bites were among my fast favorites.

   1/2 cup dry bread crumbs
   1/4 cup sesame seeds
      2 teaspoons minced fresh parsley
   1/2 cup mayonnaise
      1 teaspoon onion powder
      1 teaspoon ground mustard
   1/4 teaspoon pepper
      1 pound boneless skinless chicken breasts, cut into 1-inch cubes
      2 to 4 tablespoons vegetable oil
HONEY-MUSTARD SAUCE:
   3/4 cup mayonnaise
4-1/2 teaspoons honey
1-1/2 teaspoons Dijon mustard

In a large resealable plastic bag, combine the bread crumbs, sesame seeds and parsley; set aside. In a small bowl, combine the mayonnaise, onion powder, mustard and pepper. Coat chicken in mayonnaise mixture, then add to crumb mixture, a few pieces at a time, and shake to coat.

In a large skillet, saute chicken in oil in batches until juices run clear, adding additional oil as needed. In a small bowl, combine sauce ingredients. Serve with the chicken. **Yield:** 8-10 servings.

Sesame Chicken Bites

Calico Cheese Dip
(pictured above)
Prep/Total Time: 10 min.

Ellen Keck • Granger, Indiana
As soon as my husband tasted this tantalizing cheese dip at a party, he suggested I get the recipe...not knowing I'd already asked the hostess for it! Attractive, zesty and quick, it's truly become one of my most popular appetizers.

      4 cups (16 ounces) shredded Monterey Jack cheese
      1 can (4 ounces) chopped green chilies
      1 can (2-1/4 ounces) sliced ripe olives, drained
      4 green onions, sliced
      3 medium tomatoes, seeded and diced
   1/2 cup minced fresh parsley
      1 envelope Italian salad dressing mix
Tortilla chips

In a mixing bowl, combine the cheese, chilies, olives, onions, tomatoes and parsley. Prepare salad dressing mix according to package directions; pour over cheese mixture and mix well. Serve immediately with tortilla chips. **Yield:** 6 cups.

Frank 'n' Swiss Crescents

Simple Guacamole
Prep/Total Time: 10 min.

Heidi Main • Anchorage, Alaska
Because avocados can brown quickly, it's best to make this guacamole just before serving. If you do have to make it a little in advance, place the avocado pit in the guacamole until serving.

> 2 medium ripe avocados
> 1 tablespoon lemon juice
> 1/4 cup chunky salsa
> 1/8 to 1/4 teaspoon salt

Peel and chop avocados; place in a small bowl. Sprinkle with lemon juice. Add salsa and salt; mash coarsely with a fork. Refrigerate until serving. **Yield:** 1-1/2 cups.

Icy Lemonade
(Pictured below)
Prep/Total Time: 5 min.

Beth Stephas • Eagle Grove, Iowa
Lemon-lime soda is a wonderful way to jazz up frozen lemonade concentrate. Try it once and you'll prepare the refreshing beverage time and again.

> 1 can (12 ounces) frozen lemonade
> concentrate
> 30 ice cubes
> 4 cups lemon-lime soda, chilled

Place half of the lemonade concentrate and 12-15 ice cubes in a blender; add 2 cups soda. Cover and process on high until ice is crushed. Repeat. Serve immediately. **Yield:** 10 cups.

Frank 'n' Swiss Crescents
(Pictured above)
Prep/Total Time: 30 min.

Kids of all ages will enjoy these adorable appetizers from our Test Kitchen. The bite-size snacks are quick to assemble with convenient crescent dough, hot dogs and Swiss cheese. Serve barbecue sauce, ketchup or additional mustard alongside for dipping.

> 1 tube (8 ounces) refrigerated crescent rolls
> 2 tablespoons Dijon mustard
> 1/2 cup shredded Swiss cheese
> 1/2 teaspoon salt-free seasoning blend
> 8 hot dogs

Unroll crescent roll dough and separate into eight triangles. Cut each piece into two triangles. Spread each triangle with mustard; sprinkle with cheese and seasoning blend.

Cut rounded ends from hot dogs (discard or save for another use). Cut hot dogs in half widthwise; place one piece on the end of each triangle and roll up. Place pointed side down 2 in. apart on a baking sheet coated with nonstick cooking spray. Bake at 375° for 15-18 minutes or until golden brown. Serve warm. **Yield:** 16 appetizers.

Icy Lemonade

Peanut Cereal Squares

Prep/Total Time: 15 min.

Kathy Steffen • Fond du Lac, Wisconsin
When I need to throw together something in a hurry, I turn to these no-bake squares. And because the recipe doesn't include chocolate, you can pack them for long drives or vacations without worrying about melted-chocolate messes.

> 4 cups Rice Chex cereal
> 1 cup light corn syrup
> 1 cup sugar
> 1 cup peanut butter
> 1 cup salted peanuts
> 1 teaspoon vanilla extract

Place cereal in a greased 13-in. x 9-in. x 2-in. pan. In a saucepan, bring corn syrup and sugar to a boil; boil for 1 minute. Remove from the heat; stir in peanut butter until blended. Stir in peanuts and vanilla. Pour over cereal. Cool completely. Cut into squares. **Yield:** 2 dozen.

Brownie Kiss Cupcakes

Prep/Total Time: 30 min.

Pamela Lute • Mercersburg, Pennsylvania
It's fun to prepare individual brownie "cupcakes" with a chocolaty surprise inside. My goddaughter asks me to make them for her birthday to share at school. This year, she requested 32 of them. I increased the recipe but later found out she only needed 27 for her class...I'm quite sure I know where the extras went!

> 1/3 cup butter, softened
> 1 cup sugar
> 2 eggs
> 1 teaspoon vanilla extract
> 3/4 cup all-purpose flour
> 1/2 cup baking cocoa
> 1/4 teaspoon baking powder
> 1/4 teaspoon salt
> 9 milk chocolate kisses

In a mixing bowl, cream butter and sugar. Add eggs and vanilla; mix well. Combine flour, cocoa, baking powder and salt; add to the creamed mixture and mix well.

Fill paper- or foil-lined muffin cups two-thirds full. Place a chocolate kiss, tip end down, in the center of each. Bake at 350° for 20-25 minutes or until top of brownie springs back when lightly touched. **Yield:** 9 cupcakes.

California Fried Walnuts

California Fried Walnuts

(Pictured above)
Prep/Total Time: 25 min.

Alcy Thorne • Los Molinois, California
You only need five ingredients for these popular snacks. Tins of the walnuts also make easy hostess gifts, particularly during the holidays.

> 6 cups water
> 4 cups walnut halves
> 1/2 cup sugar
> Oil for frying
> 1-1/4 teaspoons salt

In a large saucepan, bring the water to a boil. Add the walnuts; boil for 1 minute. Drain; rinse under hot water. In a large bowl, the toss walnuts with sugar. In an electric skillet, heat 1/2 in. of oil to 350°. Fry walnuts for 5 minutes or until dark brown, stirring often. Drain in a colander over paper towels. Sprinkle with salt. Store in an airtight container. **Yield:** 4 cups.

Cheddar Herb Snacks

Prep/Total Time: 20 min.

Peggy Burdick • Burlington, Michigan
Made out of hot dog buns, these herbed rolls really hit the spot when you need a savory snack that doesn't require a lot of kitchen time.

> 6 to 8 hot dog buns
> 1 cup (4 ounces) shredded cheddar cheese
> 1/2 cup butter *or* margarine, softened
> 2 tablespoons minced fresh parsley
> 2 tablespoons minced chives
> 2 tablespoons chopped pimientos
> 1 tablespoon chopped green onion

Slice hot dog buns lengthwise. Mix remaining ingredients together; spread over the buns. Place on a baking sheet. Bake at 400° for 6-8 minutes or until cheese is melted. Cut each bun into 1-inch pieces. **Yield:** 12-16 servings.

Veggie Party Pizza

Veggie Party Pizza

(Pictured above)
Prep/Total Time: 30 min.

Laura Kadlec • Maiden Rock, Wisconsin
I originally made this yummy veggie pizza to share with a friend who was watching her cholesterol. But it's so good, I serve it to my family often. Even the kids munch on it.

> 2 cups all-purpose flour
> 2 teaspoons baking powder
> 1 teaspoon salt
> 2/3 cup fat-free milk
> 1/4 cup plus 1 tablespoon canola oil, *divided*
> TOPPING:
> 3 cups 2% cottage cheese
> 1 envelope ranch salad dressing mix
> 1/2 cup fat-free mayonnaise
> 1/4 cup fat-free milk
> 1-1/2 cups chopped fresh broccoli
> 1-1/2 cups chopped fresh cauliflower
> 1/2 cup chopped celery
> 1/3 cup shredded carrot
> 1/4 cup chopped onion
> 2 cups (8 ounces) shredded part-skim mozzarella cheese
> Sliced ripe olives, drained, optional

For crust, combine the flour, baking powder and salt. Add milk and 1/4 cup oil; mix well. Shape into a ball; knead 10 times. Press onto the bottom and up the sides of an ungreased 15-in. x 10-in. x 1-in. baking pan. Prick with fork; brush with remaining oil. Bake at 425° for 12-14 minutes or until edges are lightly browned. Cool.

In a mixing bowl, combine the cottage cheese, ranch dressing mix, mayonnaise and milk; spread over crust. Sprinkle with vegetables and cheese. Garnish with olives if desired. Refrigerate until serving. **Yield:** 14 servings.

Toasted Almond Party Spread

Prep/Total Time: 25 min.

Kim Sobota • Plymouth, Minnesota
This warm spread goes a long way at casual get-togethers and formal parties alike. Almonds and Swiss cheese are a rich combination that never goes out of style.

> 1 package (8 ounces) cream cheese, softened
> 1-1/2 cups (6 ounces) shredded Swiss cheese
> 1/2 cup sliced almonds, toasted, *divided*
> 1/3 cup mayonnaise
> 2 tablespoons sliced green onions
> 1/8 teaspoon pepper
> 1/8 teaspoon ground nutmeg
> Assorted crackers

In a small mixing bowl, beat the cream cheese until smooth. Stir in the Swiss cheese, 1/3 cup almonds, mayonnaise, onions, pepper and nutmeg. Spoon onto a lightly greased pie plate. Bake at 350° for 14-15 minutes or until heated through. Sprinkle with remaining almonds. Serve warm with crackers. **Yield:** 1-1/2 cups.

Cucumber Pita Wedges

Prep/Total Time: 10 min.

Grace Yaskovic • Branchville, New Jersey
I first tasted these delicious snacks at a party in a friend's home. Of the finger foods she served, this platter was the first to become empty!

> 1 package (8 ounces) cream cheese, softened
> 2 tablespoons Italian salad dressing mix
> 4 whole pita breads
> 1 to 2 medium cucumbers, peeled and cut into 1/8-inch slices
> Lemon-pepper seasoning

In a mixing bowl, beat cream cheese and salad dressing mix until combined. Split pita breads in half, forming two circles. Spread cream cheese mixture over pita circles; cut each into six wedges. Top with cucumbers. Sprinkle with lemon-pepper. **Yield:** 4 dozen.

Quick TIP To save even more time when preparing the dainty Cucumber Pita Wedges, leave out the salad dressing mix and purchase a tub of flavored cream cheese from the grocery store or local bagel shop.

Feta Bruschetta

Feta Bruschetta
(Pictured above)
Prep/Total Time: 30 min.

Stacey Rinehart • Eugene, Oregon
You won't believe the compliments you'll receive when you greet guests with these warm appetizers. Each crispy bite offers the savory flavors of feta cheese, tomato, basil and garlic. They're terrific for holiday parties or most any gathering.

  1/4 cup butter, melted
  1/4 cup olive oil
   10 slices French bread (1 inch thick)
    1 package (4 ounces) crumbled feta cheese
    2 to 3 garlic cloves, minced
    1 tablespoon minced fresh basil *or*
      1 teaspoon dried basil
    1 large tomato, seeded and chopped

In a small bowl, combine butter and oil; brush onto both sides of bread. Place on a baking sheet. Bake at 350° for 8-10 minutes or until lightly browned on top.

    Combine the feta cheese, garlic and basil; sprinkle over toast. Top with tomato. Bake 8-10 minutes longer or until heated through. Serve warm. **Yield:** 10 appetizers.

Easy Oat Cookies
Prep/Total Time: 15 min.

Kerry Bouchard • Shawmut, Montana
My mom used to pack these no-bake cookies into our school lunches. They're inexpensive and simple to prepare, so all seven of us children learned to make them. Now they're also a favorite of my two children.

  1/2 cup butter
  1/2 cup milk

    2 cups sugar
    3 cups dry quick-cooking *or* rolled oats
    5 tablespoons unsweetened cocoa
  1/2 cup raisins, chopped nuts *or* coconut

In a large saucepan, heat butter, milk and sugar. Bring to a boil, stirring occasionally. Boil for 1 minute. Remove from the heat. Stir in oats, cocoa and raisins, nuts or coconut. Drop by tablespoonful onto waxed paper. Cool. **Yield:** about 3 dozen cookies.

Hot 'n' Spicy Cranberry Dip
(Pictured below)
Prep/Total Time: 15 min.

Marian Platt • Sequim, Washington
When I want to make this as an appetizer on Christmas or New Year's Eve, I easily double the recipe, using one 16-ounce can of cranberry sauce.

  3/4 cup jellied cranberry sauce
    1 to 2 tablespoons prepared horseradish
    1 tablespoon honey
1-1/2 teaspoons lemon juice
1-1/2 teaspoons Worcestershire sauce
  1/8 to 1/4 teaspoon cayenne pepper
    1 garlic clove, minced
Miniature hot dogs *or* smoked sausage links, warmed
Sliced apples *or* pears

In a small saucepan, combine the first seven ingredients; bring to a boil, stirring constantly. Reduce heat. Cover and simmer for 5 minutes, stirring occasionally. Serve warm with sausage and/or fruit. **Yield:** 3/4 cup.

Hot 'n' Spicy Cranberry Dip

Chili Cheese Popcorn

Chili Cheese Popcorn

(Pictured above)
Prep/Total Time: 10 min.

Phyllis Schmalz • Kansas City, Kansas
The next time you're going on a road trip, pack some bags of this zippy popcorn snack. It comes together in minutes, and it helps the drive fly by.

  8 cups popped popcorn
1/4 cup butter, melted
1/2 teaspoon chili powder
1/4 teaspoon salt
1/2 cup grated Parmesan cheese

Place popcorn in a large bowl. Combine butter, chili powder and salt; pour over popcorn. Spread in a 15-in. x 10-in. x 1-in. baking pan; sprinkle with Parmesan cheese.

Broil 6 in. from the heat for 2-3 minutes or until the cheese is melted. Toss well to coat. Store in an airtight container. **Yield:** 2 quarts.

No-Bake Almond Bites

Prep/Total Time: 10 min.

To help keep holiday snacking on the skinny side, whip up these simple sensations from our home economists. The chewy nibbles are ideal when time is tight.

  30 vanilla wafers, finely crushed
   1 cup confectioners' sugar, *divided*
1/2 cup chopped almonds
   2 tablespoons baking cocoa
   2 tablespoons corn syrup
   2 tablespoons apple juice
1/4 teaspoon almond extract

In a large bowl, combine the wafer crumbs, 1/2 cup confectioners' sugar, almonds and cocoa. In a small bowl, combine the corn syrup, apple juice and extract. Stir into crumb mixture until well blended. Shape into 1-in. balls; roll in remaining sugar. Store in an airtight container. **Yield:** 1-1/2 dozen.

Taco Roll-ups

Prep/Total Time: 15 min.

Denice Louk • Garnett, Kansas
Our friend made these roll-ups for a Mexican-themed garden party. A sprinkling of onion soup mix makes them a little different.

  2 packages (8 ounces *each*) cream cheese, softened
  1 cup (8 ounces) sour cream
  2 cups (8 ounces) finely shredded cheddar cheese
1/2 cup picante sauce
  1 can (4-1/2 ounces) chopped ripe olives, drained
  2 tablespoons taco seasoning
  1 tablespoon onion soup mix
  8 flour tortillas (10 inches)

In a small mixing bowl, beat cream cheese and sour cream until smooth; stir in the cheddar cheese, picante sauce, olives, taco seasoning and soup mix. Spread over tortillas; roll up jelly-roll style. Wrap in plastic wrap; refrigerate for at least 1 hour. Just before serving, cut into 1-in. pieces. **Yield:** about 3-1/2 dozen.

Sweet Cereal Treats

Prep/Total Time: 20 min.

Barri VanderHulst • Allegan, Michigan
It doesn't take long to mix up a batch of these yummy goodies since they involve only four ingredients and don't require an oven. As a child, I helped my grandma make them. Now my three children enjoy helping me. We all love the crunchy treat.

5-1/3 cups Peanut Butter Captain Crunch cereal
   1 cup dry roasted peanuts
   1 package (12 ounces) vanilla baking chips
   1 tablespoon butter

In a large bowl, combine cereal and peanuts; set aside. In a microwave or double boiler, melt chips and butter; stir until smooth. Pour over cereal mixture and stir to coat. Drop by rounded tablespoonfuls onto waxed paper-lined baking sheets. Refrigerate until firm. **Yield:** about 5 dozen.

Quick TIP

Experiment with the cereal treats. Use whatever cereal your kids prefer or replace the nuts with marshmallows.

Peppery Hush Puppies

(Pictured below)
Prep/Total Time: 25 min.

Ruby Ross • Kennett, Missouri
These spicy hush puppies are as tasty an appetizer as they are a side dish to fish. They are best when they're served warm.

    2 cups cornmeal
  1/2 cup pancake mix
2-1/2 teaspoons sugar
    1 teaspoon baking powder
    1 teaspoon salt
    1 egg
    1 cup buttermilk
    2 tablespoons vegetable oil
    3 jalapeno peppers, seeded and finely
      chopped
  1/2 cup finely chopped onion
  1/8 to 1/4 teaspoon hot pepper sauce
Oil for deep-fat frying

In a bowl, combine the cornmeal, pancake mix, sugar, baking powder and salt. In another bowl, beat the egg, buttermilk, oil, jalapenos, onion and hot pepper sauce. Stir into dry ingredients just until combined.

In an electric skillet or deep-fat fryer, heat oil to 375°. Drop batter by rounded tablespoonfuls into oil. Fry for 3-4 minutes or until golden brown. Drain on paper towels. Serve warm. **Yield:** 4 dozen.

Editor's Note: When cutting or seeding hot peppers, use rubber or plastic gloves to protect your hands. Avoid touching your face.

Peppery Hush Puppies

Cheesy Zucchini Bites

Cheesy Zucchini Bites

(Pictured above)
Prep/Total Time: 30 min.

Amy Frombach • Bradford, Pennsylvania
Garden-fresh zucchini and cherry tomatoes make a great combo in these colorful hors d'oeuvres. Folks tend to hang around the appetizer tray whenever I serve these pretty, party bites.

    5 medium zucchini (about 6 inches long)
    4 ounces blue cheese, crumbled
    3 tablespoons grated Parmesan cheese
    1 teaspoon dried basil
  1/8 teaspoon pepper
    1 pint cherry tomatoes, thinly sliced

Cut zucchini into 3/4-in. slices. Using a melon baller or small spoon, scoop out the insides and discard, leaving the bottom intact. Place zucchini on an ungreased baking sheet; spoon 1/2 teaspoon crumbled blue cheese into each.

Combine Parmesan cheese, basil and pepper; sprinkle half over blue cheese. Top each with a tomato slice; sprinkle with remaining Parmesan mixture.

Bake at 400° for 5-7 minutes or until cheese is melted. Serve warm. **Yield:** 35 appetizers.

Cherry Cranberry Shakes

Prep/Total Time: 10 min.

Gayle Lewis • Yucaipa, California
Here's a change-of-pace drink great for fall. The combination of cranberry juice and cherry soda is tongue tingling.

    1 cup cranberry juice, chilled
    1 cup cherry soda, chilled
    1 tablespoon milk *or* half-and-half cream
  3/4 teaspoon vanilla extract
    1 cup vanilla ice cream, softened

Place all of the ingredients in a blender; cover and process until smooth. Pour into chilled glasses. **Yield:** 3-1/2 cups.

Layered Roast Beef Salad, BLT Soup
And Summer Sub Sandwich (p. 30)

Swift Soups, Salads & Sandwiches

For time-saving convenience, few foods compare to chill-chasing soups, garden-fresh salads or sandwiches piled high with flavor. Try one of these fast favorites today!

Tangy Vegetable Pasta Salad

(Pictured below)
Prep/Total Time: 30 min.

Wilma Jones • Mobile, Alabama
The variety of ingredients in my pasta salad will take your taste buds in all different directions. It's surprising how well the zesty citrus and strong vegetable flavors blend together.

    2-1/4 cups uncooked spiral pasta
        2 tablespoons lemon juice
        3 plum tomatoes, sliced
      1/2 cup chopped green pepper
      1/2 cup radish slices
      1/2 cup chopped peeled cucumber
DRESSING:
      1/3 cup picante V8 juice
      1/4 cup orange juice
        2 tablespoons lemon juice
        2 tablespoons chopped green onion
        1 tablespoon canola oil
    1-1/2 teaspoons sugar
        1 teaspoon grated lemon peel
        1 teaspoon grated orange peel
      1/2 teaspoon salt
      1/2 teaspoon dill weed

Cook pasta according to package directions, adding the lemon juice to the water the directions call for. Drain and cool.

In a large bowl, combine the pasta, tomatoes, green pepper, radishes and cucumber. In a jar with a tight-fitting lid, combine the dressing ingredients; shake well. Pour over salad; toss to coat. Cover and refrigerate until serving. **Yield:** 6 servings.

Tangy Vegetable Pasta Salad

Red Potato Salad

Prep/Total Time: 10 min.

Susan Martin • Hollis, New Hampshire
I created this ultra-fast recipe while trying to find an alternative to the usual potato salad. Its flavor might remind you of a baked potato with toppings such as sour cream, cheddar cheese and crumbled bacon.

        7 medium red potatoes, cooked and cubed
      1/4 cup sour cream
      1/4 cup mayonnaise
      1/4 cup shredded cheddar cheese
        2 tablespoons chopped red onion
        1 bacon strip, cooked and crumbled
    1-1/2 teaspoons minced chives
Salt and pepper to taste

In a large bowl, combine all of the ingredients. Refrigerate until serving. **Yield:** 4-6 servings.

Deluxe Bacon Burgers

Prep/Total Time: 20 min.

Bernadine Dirmeyer • Harpster, Ohio
I created this recipe and even won a ribbon for it in a contest. Perfect for busy nights, it's like meat loaf in a bun. It's very tasty. Sometimes I serve it with gravy and leave the bun out completely. Top the burgers with tomato slices, cheese or mayonnaise if you'd like.

        2 large carrots, grated
        1 large onion, grated
        1 cup mashed potato flakes
        2 eggs, lightly beaten
        1 garlic clove, minced
        1 teaspoon salt
Pepper to taste
        2 pounds ground beef
        8 bacon strips
        8 lettuce leaves, optional
        8 hamburger buns, split, optional

In a large bowl, combine the first seven ingredients. Crumble beef over mixture and mix gently. Shape into eight patties. Wrap a bacon strip around each patty; secure with toothpicks.

In a large skillet, cook burgers until meat is no longer pink and bacon is crisp. Remove toothpicks. Serve burgers on lettuce-lined buns if desired. **Yield:** 8 servings.

Crunchy Coleslaw
Fancy Ham 'n' Cheese

In a small saucepan, heat oil. Stir in contents of noodle seasoning packet and garlic salt; cook for 3-4 minutes or until blended.

Meanwhile, crush the noodles and place in a large salad bowl. Add coleslaw mix and almonds. Drizzle with oil mixture; toss to coat. Serve immediately. **Yield:** 6-8 servings.

Fancy Ham 'n' Cheese

(Pictured above)
Prep/Total Time: 10 min.

James Gauthier • Oak Creek, Wisconsin
Garden-fresh ingredients including spinach, cucumber and onion add appeal to this zippy ham sandwich. It has a touch of class that quickly turns the ordinary into something special.

    1/4 cup butter, softened
      8 slices rye bread
     12 fresh spinach leaves
     16 cucumber slices
      4 thin slices red onion
     12 slices fully cooked ham
      2 tablespoons Dijon mustard
      8 slices cheddar cheese

Spread butter on one side of each slice of bread. On half of the slices, layer spinach, cucumber, onion, ham, mustard and cheese. Top with remaining bread. **Yield:** 4 servings.

Crunchy Coleslaw

(Pictured above)
Prep/Total Time: 10 min.

Julie Vavroch • Montezuma, Iowa
This crunchy, five-item salad is so simple to put together that we often have it for spur-of-the-moment picnics or when unexpected guests stop by. It gets its nutty flavor from almonds.

    1/3 cup vegetable oil
      1 package (3 ounces) beef ramen noodles
    1/2 teaspoon garlic salt
      1 package (16 ounces) shredded coleslaw mix
      1 package (5 ounces) sliced almonds

Too-Easy Tortellini Soup

DISH MEAL

(Pictured below)
Prep/Total Time: 20 min.

Beth Daley • Chesterfield, Missouri
For a hearty soup, I turn packaged tortellini and canned goods into a minute-made dinner. Basil and Parmesan cheese round out the flavor of this wonderfully easy recipe.

      4 cups chicken broth
      1 package (9 ounces) refrigerated cheese
         tortellini
      1 can (15 ounces) white kidney *or* cannellini
         beans, rinsed and drained
      1 can (14-1/2 ounces) Italian diced
         tomatoes, undrained
  1-1/2 teaspoons dried basil
      1 tablespoon red wine vinegar
Shredded Parmesan cheese and coarsely ground
    pepper, optional

In a large saucepan, bring broth to a boil. Stir in tortellini. Reduce heat; simmer, uncovered, for 4 minutes, stirring occasionally. Stir in the beans, tomatoes and basil. Simmer for 4-6 minutes or until pasta is tender. Stir in the vinegar. Sprinkle with Parmesan cheese and pepper if desired. **Yield:** 6 servings.

Too-Easy Tortellini Soup

Sausage Chicken Soup

Sausage Chicken Soup
(Pictured above)
Prep/Total Time: 30 min.

Helen MacDonald • Lazo, British Columbia
I've been making this satisfying soup for years, but my husband is still thrilled whenever I put it on the table. Made in half an hour, it's loaded with slices of smoked sausage, chunks of chicken, fresh peppers and hearty potatoes. Spice it up or tone it down with your family's favorite picante sauce.

> 3/4 pound boneless skinless chicken breasts
> 2 medium potatoes, peeled and cut into 1/4-inch cubes
> 1 can (14-1/2 ounces) chicken broth
> 1 medium onion, diced
> 1 medium sweet red pepper, diced
> 1 medium green pepper, diced
> 1 garlic clove, minced
> 3/4 cup picante sauce
> 3 tablespoons all-purpose flour
> 3 tablespoons water
> 1/2 pound smoked sausage, diced
> Sliced habanero peppers, optional

Place chicken in a greased microwave-safe dish. Cover and microwave on high for 5-7 minutes or until juices run clear, turning every 2 minutes. Cut into cubes; set aside.

Place potatoes and broth in a 2-1/2-qt. microwave-safe bowl. Cover and microwave on high for 5 minutes. Add the onions, peppers and garlic; cook 5 minutes longer or until potatoes are tender. Stir in the picante sauce.

In a small bowl, combine the flour and water until smooth. Add to the potato mixture. Cover and cook on high for 3 minutes or until thickened. Add chicken and sausage; cook 1-2 minutes longer or until heated through. Sprinkle with habaneros if desired. **Yield:** 6 servings.

Editor's Note: This recipe was tested with an 850-watt microwave.

Pork Tenderloin Sandwiches
Prep/Total Time: 15 min.

Margarete Muhle • Pewaukee, Wisconsin
Chutney and pears add a distinctive touch to these open-faced sandwiches, making them perfect for special luncheons. They're so simple, however, that you won't mind making them regularly.

> 2 pork tenderloins (about 1 pound *each*), trimmed
> 1 teaspoon seasoned salt
> 1/2 teaspoon pepper
> 1 to 2 tablespoons olive oil
> 6 slices sourdough bread
> 3 tablespoons mango chutney
> 1 can (15 ounces) sliced pears, drained
> 6 slices process American cheese

Cut pork crosswise into six slices; sprinkle with seasoned salt and pepper. Flatten to 1/4-in. thickness; cook in oil in a large skillet over medium heat for about 4 minutes per side or until no longer pink.

Meanwhile, toast bread and spread each slice with about 2 teaspoons chutney. Top with tenderloin, pears and cheese; place on an ungreased baking sheet. Bake at 300° for 2-3 minutes or until cheese is melted. **Yield:** 6 servings.

Mozzarella Tuna Melts
(Pictured below)
Prep/Total Time: 30 min.

Jo Maasberg • Farson, Wyoming
Our daughter's home economics teacher shared the recipe for these warm, all-American bites. Using a mini food processor to chop the celery and onion for the filling cuts down on prep time. Then, we just pop the sandwiches in the oven.

> 1 can (6 ounces) water-packed tuna, drained and flaked
> 1/4 cup finely chopped celery
> 1/4 cup finely chopped onion
> 1/4 cup mayonnaise

Mozzarella Tuna Melts

4 hamburger buns, split
4 slices part-skim mozzarella cheese
4 tomato slices
4 lettuce leaves

In a small bowl, combine the tuna, celery, onion and mayonnaise. Spread on bottom of buns; set bun tops aside. Top tuna mixture with a slice of cheese and tomato.

Place on an ungreased baking sheet. Bake, uncovered, at 350° for 12-15 minutes or until heated through and cheese is melted. Top each with a lettuce leaf; replace bun tops. **Yield:** 4 servings.

Greens with Herb Dressing
Prep/Total Time: 10 min.

Marian Platt • Sequim, Washington
Looking for a different salad dressing? Consider this light, savory herb variety. It's a fast, refreshing topper for any combination of salad greens.

6 tablespoons olive oil
2 tablespoons red wine vinegar
2 teaspoons Dijon mustard
1 teaspoon minced fresh tarragon *or*
   1/4 teaspoon dried tarragon
1 teaspoon minced fresh thyme *or*
   1/4 teaspoon dried thyme
2 teaspoons lemon *or* lime juice
2 garlic cloves, minced
1/4 teaspoon salt
Dash pepper
8 cups torn mixed salad greens

In a jar with tight-fitting lid, combine the first nine ingredients; shake well. Place the greens in salad bowl. Drizzle with dressing; toss to coat. Serve immediately. **Yield:** 8 servings.

Zippy Egg Salad
Prep/Total Time: 10 min.

Annemarie Pietila • Farmington Hills, Michigan
Egg salad is always a tasty change from lunch meat or peanut butter sandwiches. Everyone raves about this swift version with its touch of mustard and lemon juice.

3 tablespoons mayonnaise
1-1/2 teaspoons prepared mustard
1/8 teaspoon salt
1/8 teaspoon pepper
1/8 teaspoon lemon juice
3 hard-cooked eggs, coarsely chopped
1 tablespoon minced green onion
Bread *or* crackers
Sliced tomato, optional

White Chili with Chicken

In a small bowl, combine the mayonnaise, mustard, salt, pepper and lemon juice. Stir in the eggs and onion. Serve on bread or crackers; top with tomato if desired. **Yield:** 2 servings.

White Chili With Chicken

(Pictured above)
Prep/Total Time: 30 min.

Christy Campos • Richmond, Virginia
Those who enjoy a change from tomato-based chili will take to this easy recipe. The flavorful blend has tender chunks of chicken, white beans and just enough flair to keep folks coming back for seconds.

1 medium onion, chopped
1 jalapeno pepper, seeded and chopped, optional
2 garlic cloves, minced
1 tablespoon vegetable oil
4 cups chicken broth
2 cans (15-1/2 ounces *each*) great northern beans, rinsed and drained
2 tablespoons minced fresh parsley
1 tablespoon lime juice
1 to 1-1/4 teaspoons ground cumin
2 tablespoons cornstarch
1/4 cup cold water
2 cups cubed cooked chicken

In a large saucepan, cook the onion, jalapeno if desired and garlic in oil until tender. Stir in the broth, beans, parsley, lime juice and cumin; bring to a boil. Reduce heat; cover and simmer for 10 minutes, stirring occasionally.

Combine cornstarch and water until smooth; stir into chili. Add chicken. Bring to a boil; cook and stir for 2 minutes or until thickened. **Yield:** 6 servings.

Editor's Note: When cutting or seeding hot peppers, use rubber or plastic gloves to protect your hands. Avoid touching your face.

Chili in No Time

Prep/Total Time: 30 min.

Pearl Johnson • Prior Lake, Minnesota
A handful of ingredients are all you need for this weeknight chili. After just one taste, you'll turn to the recipe time and again.

- 1-1/2 pounds ground beef
- 1 medium onion, chopped
- 1 can (28 ounces) crushed tomatoes
- 1 jar (30 ounces) spaghetti sauce
- 2 cans (16 ounces *each*) kidney beans
- 2 to 4 tablespoons chili powder

In a large kettle or Dutch oven, brown beef and onion; drain. Add remaining ingredients; simmer for at least 15 minutes, stirring occasionally. **Yield:** 10 servings (2-1/2 quarts).

BLT Soup

(Pictured on page 24)
Prep/Total Time: 20 min.

Sharon Richardson • Dallas, Texas
The BLT is a family favorite, so I came up with a soup that has all the fabulous flavor of the sandwich.

- 3 tablespoons butter
- 2 teaspoons vegetable oil
- 3 cups cubed French bread
- 1 pound sliced bacon, diced
- 2 cups finely chopped celery
- 1 medium onion, finely chopped
- 2 tablespoons sugar
- 6 tablespoons all-purpose flour
- 5 cups chicken broth
- 1 jar (16 ounces) picante sauce
- 1 can (8 ounces) tomato sauce
- 1/8 teaspoon pepper
- 3 cups shredded lettuce

In a Dutch oven or large saucepan, heat butter and oil over medium heat. Add the bread cubes; stir until crisp and golden brown. Remove and set aside. In the same pan, cook bacon until crisp. Drain, reserving 1/4 cup drippings; set bacon aside.

Saute celery and onion in drippings until tender. Add sugar; cook and stir for 1 minute or until sugar is dissolved. Gradually stir in flour; cook and stir for 1 minute or until blended. Add broth, picante sauce, tomato sauce and pepper; bring to a boil. Boil and stir for 2 minutes or until thickened.

Just before serving, add lettuce and heat through. Sprinkle with croutons and bacon. **Yield:** 8 servings (2 quarts).

Summer Sub Sandwich

(Pictured on page 24)
Prep/Total Time: 10 min.

Jennifer Beck • Concord, Ohio
We love submarine sandwiches, so I came up with this ham-and-cheese combination. It's good served either hot or cold, and it doesn't keep me in the kitchen long.

- 1 loaf (1 pound) unsliced French bread
- 1 package (3 ounces) cream cheese, softened
- 8 slices fully cooked ham
- 6 slices provolone cheese
- 1 jar (4 ounces) sliced mushrooms, drained
- 1-1/2 cups shredded lettuce
- 2 medium tomatoes, thinly sliced
- 1 small onion, thinly sliced
- 2 banana peppers, thinly sliced

Cut the loaf of bread in half horizontally. Spread bottom half with cream cheese; layer with ham, provolone and mushrooms. Replace top.

Cut loaf in half; wrap in paper towels. Microwave on high for 45-60 seconds. Remove top; add lettuce, tomatoes, onion and peppers. Replace top. Cut into serving-size pieces. **Yield:** 4 servings.

Editor's Note: When cutting or seeding hot peppers, use rubber or plastic gloves to protect your hands. Avoid touching your face.

Layered Roast Beef Salad

(Pictured on page 24)
Prep/Total Time: 15 min.

Susan Graham • Cherokee, Iowa
I've prepared this fast-to-fix salad for my bridge club several times, and I always get requests for the recipe. It's an entree salad that can't be beat. If I don't have leftover roast beef on hand, I use sliced roast beef from the deli with equally tasty results.

- 8 cups torn mixed salad greens
- 1 pound sliced deli roast beef, cut into 3/4-inch strips
- 1 cup grated carrots
- 1/2 cup thinly sliced red onion
- 3 hard-cooked eggs, sliced
- 1 cup (8 ounces) sour cream *or* plain yogurt
- 1/2 cup mayonnaise
- 1 tablespoon minced fresh parsley
- 1 tablespoon minced fresh basil

In a large salad bowl, layer a third of the greens, beef, carrots, onion and eggs. Repeat layers twice. Combine remaining ingredients; spread over salad. Toss just before serving. **Yield:** 6-8 servings.

Creamy Cashew
Chicken Salad

Creamy Cashew Chicken Salad

(Pictured above)
Prep/Total Time: 20 min.

Sara Laker • Loda, Illinois
Served on a bed of garden greens or on a croissant, this all-time classic is loaded with chicken and cashews. The nuts add a pleasant crunch and make it company-special without much effort.

      4 cups cubed cooked chicken
      1 cup chopped celery
   1/2 cup chopped green pepper
      1 jar (2 ounces) diced pimientos, drained
   1/2 cup mayonnaise
   1/3 cup heavy whipping cream
   1/4 cup sour cream
      3 tablespoons thinly sliced green onions
      2 tablespoons minced fresh parsley
1-1/2 teaspoons lemon juice
1-1/2 teaspoons tarragon vinegar
      1 garlic clove, minced
   1/2 teaspoon salt
   1/8 teaspoon pepper
   3/4 cup salted cashews
Leaf lettuce and additional cashews, optional

In a large bowl, combine the chicken, celery, green pepper and pimientos; set aside.

In a blender, combine the next 10 ingredients; cover and process until well blended. Pour over chicken mixture; toss to coat. Cover and refrigerate until serving.

Just before serving fold in cashews. Serve in a lettuce-lined bowl if desired. Sprinkle with additional cashews if desired. **Yield:** 6 servings.

Turkey Divan Croissants

(Pictured below)
Prep/Total Time: 20 min.

Ann Pirrung • Cleveland, Wisconsin
I always served these tasty sandwiches at ladies' luncheons. One time I had leftovers and discovered my fussy family enjoyed them, too.

   1/3 cup mayonnaise
   1/4 cup Dijon mustard
1-1/2 teaspoons lemon juice
   1/2 teaspoon dill weed
      1 pound broccoli, finely chopped
   1/2 cup chopped onion
      2 tablespoons butter
      1 cup sliced fresh mushrooms
      6 croissants, split
      6 ounces thinly sliced cooked turkey
      6 slices Swiss cheese

In a small bowl, combine mayonnaise, mustard, lemon juice and dill; set aside.

In a large skillet, saute broccoli and onion in butter for 10 minutes or until tender. Add mushrooms; cook and stir until tender.

Spread mustard mixture over bottom halves of croissants. Top with turkey, broccoli mixture and cheese; replace tops.

Place on a baking sheet. Bake at 350° for 5 minutes or until heated through and cheese is melted. **Yield:** 6 servings.

Turkey Divan Croissants

Sweet Sesame Salad

Sweet Sesame Salad

(Pictured above)
Prep/Total Time: 30 min.

Kristine Marra • Clifton Park, New York
Packaged greens and a bottled salad dressing give me a head start on this salad. Mandarin oranges and sesame seeds lend a special touch.

>   1 package (10 ounces) ready-to-serve salad
>   greens
>   1 medium tomato, cut into thin wedges
>   2/3 cup balsamic vinaigrette salad dressing
>   2 teaspoons honey
>   1 can (11 ounces) mandarin oranges, drained
>   1 teaspoon sesame seeds, toasted

In a large salad bowl, combine the greens and tomato; set aside. In a jar with a tight-fitting lid, combine salad dressing and honey; shake well. Drizzle over greens. Sprinkle with oranges and sesame seeds; toss to coat. **Yield:** 6 servings.

Zucchini Bisque

Prep/Total Time: 30 min.

Marjorie Beck • Sonora, California
I like to serve this soup as a first course for weekend dinners. It is nice and light, pretty in color and very appetizing with its blend of flavors.

>   1 medium onion, diced
>   1/2 cup butter, cubed
> 2-1/2 cups shredded zucchini
> 2-1/2 cups chicken broth
>   1/2 teaspoon dried basil
>   1/2 teaspoon salt
>   1/2 teaspoon pepper
>   1/4 teaspoon ground nutmeg
>   1 cup half-and-half cream

In a large saucepan, saute onion in butter. Add zucchini and chicken broth. Simmer, covered, for about 15 minutes; add seasonings.

Puree on low in a blender. Return to pan; stir in cream and heat through. **Yield:** 4-5 servings (5 cups).

Corn Bread Salad

Prep/Total Time: 25 min.

Sherry Edwards • Camden, Arkansas
This recipe appeared in our local newspaper years ago, and I adapted it to suit our tastes. My husband is a great cook, and we've been sharing the kitchen since his retirement. This is a favorite of both of ours.

>   3/4 pound ground beef
> 1-1/2 cups crumbled corn bread
>   1 can (15 ounces) pinto beans, rinsed and
>   drained
>   2 celery ribs, chopped
>   1 large onion, chopped
>   4 medium tomatoes, chopped

TOPPING:
> 1-1/3 cups mayonnaise
>   2 teaspoons sugar
>   2 teaspoons vinegar

In a large skillet, cook beef over medium heat until no longer pink; drain and cool slightly.

In a large bowl, layer corn bread, beans, celery, onion and tomatoes. Spoon beef over tomato layer. In a small bowl, combine the mayonnaise, sugar and vinegar. Spread topping over salad (do not toss). **Yield:** 8 servings.

Fried Green Tomato Sandwiches

Prep/Total Time: 20 min.

Mary Ann Bostic • Sinks Grove, West Virginia
Here is one of my best quick-to-fix suppers. If you've never tried fried green tomatoes, give them a shot! They're yummy in these sandwiches.

>   1/4 cup all-purpose flour
>   1/4 teaspoon *each* garlic powder, salt, pepper
>   and paprika
>   3 medium green tomatoes, sliced
>   12 bacon strips
>   12 slices sourdough bread, toasted
>   6 slices provolone cheese
> Leaf lettuce, mayonnaise and Dijon mustard

In a shallow dish, combine flour and seasonings; dip tomatoes in the mixture and set aside. In a large skillet, cook bacon over medium heat until crisp.

Remove to paper towels to drain. In the drippings, cook tomatoes for 2 minutes on each side; drain on paper towels.

Place six slices of toast on a baking sheet. Layer with three tomato slices, two bacon strips and a cheese slice. Broil 3-4 in. from the heat for 3-4 minutes or until cheese is melted. Top with lettuce if desired.

Spread mayonnaise and mustard on remaining toast if desired; place over lettuce. **Yield:** 6 sandwiches.

BLT Macaroni Salad

(Pictured below)
Prep/Total Time: 30 min.

Mrs. Hamilton Myers Jr. • Charlottesville, Virginia
A friend served this salad, and I just had to get the recipe. My husband enjoys BLT sandwiches, so this has become a favorite of his. It's nice to serve on hot and humid days or when you're in a hurry.

> 1/2 cup mayonnaise
>   3 tablespoons chili sauce
>   2 tablespoons lemon juice
>   1 teaspoon sugar
>   3 cups cooked elbow macaroni
> 1/2 cup chopped seeded tomato
>   2 tablespoons chopped green onions
>   3 cups shredded lettuce
>   4 bacon strips, cooked and crumbled

In a large bowl, combine the first four ingredients. Add the macaroni, tomatoes and onions; toss to coat. Cover and refrigerate. Just before serving, add lettuce and bacon; toss to coat. **Yield:** 6 servings.

Meatball Minestrone

Meatball Minestrone

(Pictured above)
Prep/Total Time: 30 min.

Linda de Beaudrap • Calgary, Alberta
As the busy parents of two boys, my husband and I are always on the lookout for quick meals. You don't have to thaw frozen meatballs for this satisfying soup, so it's table-ready in just a half hour.

> 6 cups water
> 1 can (16 ounces) kidney beans, rinsed and drained
> 1 package (16 ounces) frozen mixed vegetables
> 2 tablespoons beef bouillon granules
> 1 tablespoon dried minced onion
> 1 bay leaf
> 1 teaspoon dried basil
> 1 teaspoon salt
> 1/2 teaspoon pepper
> 4 ounces spaghetti, broken into 2-inch pieces
> 24 cooked meatballs
> 1 can (14-1/2 ounces) stewed tomatoes

In a Dutch oven or soup kettle, combine the first nine ingredients. Bring to a boil; add spaghetti. Reduce heat; cover and simmer for 10 minutes or until spaghetti is tender. Add the meatballs and tomatoes; heat through. Discard bay leaf. **Yield:** 10-12 servings.

BLT Macaroni Salad

Quick TIP Take advantage of last night's extras to streamline this evening's soup. Adding leftover veggies and meats to soup not only increases flavor, but they make a fast and easy way to bulk up any soup recipe.

Garden Primavera (p. 39)

Chapter 4

Streamlined Side Dishes

Serving a perfect dinner accompaniment has never been easier than it is with the savory specialties in this chapter. Consider these tasty ideas, many of which are ready in less than 30 minutes.

Broccoli Supreme

(Pictured below)
Prep/Total Time: 30 min.

Maretta Ballinger • Visalia, California
Here's a creamy side dish that goes well with many entrees. It's a breeze to make and can even be made ahead of time. It's a tasty way to dress up broccoli with hardly any effort.

> 1 package (16 ounces) frozen chopped broccoli, thawed and drained
> 1 can (10-3/4 ounces) condensed cream of mushroom soup, undiluted
> 1/2 cup sour cream
> 1/2 cup chopped celery
> 1 jar (2 ounces) diced pimientos, drained
> 1/2 teaspoon salt
> 1/2 teaspoon pepper
> 1/2 cup shredded cheddar cheese

In a large bowl, combine the first seven ingredients; stir to coat. Transfer to a greased 1-1/2-qt. baking dish. Sprinkle with cheese. Bake, uncovered, at 350° for 20 minutes or until heated through. **Yield:** 4-6 servings.

Broccoli Supreme

Confetti Couscous

Prep/Total Time: 15 min.

Marla Stewart • Kirby, Arkansas
Couscous prepared this way makes a fun side dish alongside chicken, pork or fish. I've also stirred in pineapple chunks and cooked chicken for a great, no-hassle lunch.

> 1 can (14-1/2 ounces) chicken broth
> 2 tablespoons water
> 2 tablespoons lemon juice
> 1 teaspoon grated lemon peel
> 1/2 teaspoon salt
> 1 package (10 ounces) couscous
> 2 cups frozen peas, thawed
> 1/2 cup slivered almonds, toasted
> 1 jar (4 ounces) diced pimientos, drained

In a saucepan, bring the broth, water, lemon juice, peel and salt to a boil. Stir in couscous and peas. Cover; remove from the heat and let stand for 5 minutes. Stir in the almonds and the pimientos. **Yield:** 6 servings.

Corn Rice Medley

Prep/Total Time: 25 min.

Cheryl Ivers • Orangeburg, South Carolina
Adding vegetables to rice is a simple way to dress it up, and this side dish proves that. It's a cinch to toss together, allowing you time to tend to the rest of your meal.

> 1 cup chicken broth
> 1/2 cup uncooked long grain rice
> 1/4 cup chopped sweet red pepper
> 1 green onion, chopped
> 1 tablespoon olive oil
> 1/2 cup frozen corn, thawed
> 1 tablespoon grated Parmesan cheese

In a large saucepan, bring broth to a boil; add rice. Reduce heat; cover and simmer for 10 minutes.

Meanwhile, in a small skillet, saute the red pepper and green onion in oil until tender. Stir into rice. Add the corn. Cover and cook for 5 minutes or until rice is tender. Sprinkle with Parmesan cheese. **Yield:** 2 servings.

Honey-Garlic Angel Hair

Prep/Total Time: 10 min.

Terri Frabotta • Sterling Heights, Michigan
I received this recipe from the captain of our fire department. It's a fast favorite that's nicely seasoned with garlic and basil while offering a subtle sweetness from honey.

1 package (16 ounces) angel hair pasta
2 to 3 garlic cloves, minced
1/2 cup butter, cubed
1/4 cup honey
1 teaspoon dried basil
1 teaspoon dried thyme
1/4 cup grated Parmesan cheese

Cook pasta according to package directions. Meanwhile, in a skillet, saute the garlic in butter. Stir in the honey, basil and thyme. Drain pasta; add to garlic mixture and toss to coat. Sprinkle with Parmesan cheese. **Yield:** 8 servings.

Gingered Squash Saute
(Pictured below)
Prep/Total Time: 20 min.

Ruth Andrewson • Leavenworth, Washington
This vibrant veggie saute puts summer's bounty in the spotlight. The recipe comes from a 20-year-old cookbook, but I still use it, especially when produce from our garden is plentiful.

1 pound yellow summer squash
1/2 pound small zucchini, sliced
1 medium onion, thinly sliced
1 medium green pepper, julienned
4 teaspoons butter
3 medium tomatoes, peeled and quartered
3/4 teaspoon salt
1/2 to 1 teaspoon ground ginger

Cut yellow squash in half lengthwise, then into 1/2-in. slices. In a large skillet, saute squash, zucchini, onion and green peppers for 3 minutes. Add tomatoes, salt and ginger. Cover and cook 2-3 minutes or until heated through. **Yield:** 9 servings.

Gingered Squash Saute

Saucy Green Bean Bake

Saucy Green Bean Bake
(Pictured above)
Prep/Total Time: 30 min.

June Formanek • Belle Plaine, Iowa
Here's a different way to serve green beans. It's a nice change of pace from plain vegetables yet doesn't require much work on your part. Keep it in mind the next time your schedule is full but you still want to set a dinner on the table.

1 can (8 ounces) tomato sauce
2 tablespoons diced pimientos
1 tablespoon prepared mustard
1/4 teaspoon salt
1/8 teaspoon pepper
1 pound fresh *or* frozen cut green beans, cooked
1/2 cup chopped onion
1/3 cup chopped green pepper
1 garlic clove, minced
2 tablespoons butter
3/4 cup shredded process cheese (Velveeta)

In a large bowl, combine the first five ingredients. Add the green beans; toss to coat. Transfer to an ungreased 1-qt. baking dish. Cover and bake at 350° for 20 minutes.

Meanwhile, in a large skillet, saute onion, green pepper and garlic in butter until tender. Sprinkle over beans. Top with cheese. Bake, uncovered, for 3 minutes or until cheese is melted. **Yield:** 4-6 servings.

Hearty Bean Side Dish

Hearty Bean Side Dish
(Pictured above)
Prep/Total Time: 30 min.

Tina Roberts • Wellington, Ohio
I prepared this comforting, down-home dish to share at a family wedding. It was well received, and no one believed how easy it was to assemble.

> 1 pound fully cooked smoked sausage links, sliced
> 1 can (28 ounces) pork and beans, undrained
> 1 can (16 ounces) kidney beans, rinsed and drained
> 1 can (15-1/2 ounces) chili beans in chili sauce, undrained
> 1 can (15 ounces) lima beans, drained
> 1 can (14-1/2 ounces) cut green beans, drained
> 1 can (14-1/2 ounces) condensed tomato soup, undiluted
> 1 can (6 ounces) tomato paste
> 1/2 cup packed brown sugar
> 1/2 cup barbecue sauce

In a Dutch oven or soup kettle, combine all ingredients. Bring to a boil. Reduce heat; cover and simmer for 20 minutes or until heated through. **Yield:** 16-20 servings.

Barley and Rice Pilaf
Prep/Total Time: 20 min.

Marilyn Bazant • Albuquerque, New Mexico
If you're tired of potatoes, try this quick-and-easy pilaf for a change of pace. I put it together one night while trying to use up leftover rice. I've experimented with many variations, such as adding broccoli and asparagus, so feel free to get creative with it.

> 1/2 cup finely chopped celery
> 1/2 cup finely chopped sweet red pepper
> 1/2 cup finely chopped green onions
> 1 garlic clove, minced
> 1 tablespoon vegetable oil
> 3 cups cooked long grain rice
> 1 cup cooked medium pearl barley
> 2 bacon strips, cooked and crumbled
> 1/2 teaspoon salt
> 1/8 teaspoon pepper

In a large skillet, saute the celery, red pepper, onions and garlic in oil until crisp-tender. Stir in the rice, barley, bacon, salt and pepper; cook and stir until heated through. **Yield:** 6 servings.

Mixed Beans with Lime Butter
(Pictured below)
Prep/Total Time: 20 min.

Lois Fetting • Nelson, Wisconsin
Here's a simple yet delicious way to showcase green and wax beans. I think the recipe is best with beans fresh from your garden or the farmers market.

> 1/2 pound *each* fresh green and wax beans, trimmed
> 2 tablespoons butter
> 2 teaspoons snipped fresh dill
> 2 teaspoons lime juice
> 1 teaspoon grated lime peel
> 1/2 teaspoon salt
> 1/4 teaspoon pepper

Place beans in saucepan and cover with water; bring to a boil. Cook, uncovered, for 10 minutes or until crisp-tender; drain.

Melt butter in a skillet; add the dill, lime juice and peel, salt, pepper and beans. Stir to coat and cook until heated through. **Yield:** 4 servings.

Mixed Beans with Lime Butter

Garden Primavera

(Pictured on page 34)
Prep/Total Time: 30 min.

Ann Heinonen • Howell, Michigan
I made several changes to the original recipe for this pasta and vegetable toss to better suit our family's tastes. With its pretty color and fresh flavor, it even makes a great meatless main course.

    8 ounces uncooked fettuccine
    1 cup fresh broccoli florets
    1 medium sweet red pepper, julienned
  1/2 cup sliced carrot
  1/2 cup sliced mushrooms
  1/4 cup sliced celery
    1 garlic clove, minced
    1 tablespoon olive oil
  3/4 cup V8 juice
  1/4 cup chopped fresh basil
    1 cup frozen peas, thawed
  1/2 teaspoon salt
  1/8 teaspoon pepper
    2 tablespoons shredded Parmesan cheese

Cook fettuccine according to package directions.

Meanwhile, in a large nonstick skillet, saute the broccoli, red pepper, carrot, mushrooms, celery and garlic in oil for 3 minutes. Add V8 juice and basil. Reduce heat; simmer, uncovered, for 3 minutes. Stir in the peas, salt and pepper; simmer 2 minutes longer or until peas are tender.

Drain the fettuccine; add to vegetable mixture and toss to coat. Sprinkle with Parmesan cheese. **Yield:** 4 servings.

Creamy Corn

Prep/Total Time: 30 min.

Carol White • Vernona, Illinois
I make this recipe often because it only takes minutes to prepare on the stove and really hits the spot on chilly or rainy days. Cheese and cream-style corn turn a package of seasoned noodles into a hearty sensation.

    1 package (4.3 ounces) quick-cooking noodles and butter herb sauce mix
    1 can (14-3/4 ounces) cream-style corn
    2 ounces process cheese (Velveeta), cubed

Prepare noodles and sauce mix according to package directions. When the noodles are tender, stir in corn and cheese; cook and stir until cheese is melted. Let stand for 5 minutes. **Yield:** 6-8 servings.

Asparagus with Orange Sauce

Asparagus with Orange Sauce

(Pictured above)
Prep/Total Time: 20 min.

Lucy Meyring • Walden, Colorado
Pretty enough for weekend guests but simple enough for weeknights, this asparagus dish has a delightful citrus flavor. You can rely on it to spruce up nearly any main course.

 1-1/2 pounds fresh asparagus, trimmed
    1 garlic clove, quartered
    3 tablespoons butter
  1/4 cup orange juice
    2 tablespoons grated orange peel
  1/4 teaspoon salt
  1/8 teaspoon pepper
    1 medium navel orange, peeled and sectioned

Place asparagus and a small amount of water in a large skillet; bring to a boil. Cover and cook for 6-8 minutes or until crisp-tender.

Meanwhile, in another skillet, saute garlic in butter for 1 minute; discard garlic. Stir in the orange juice, peel, salt and pepper; heat through.

Drain asparagus and place in a serving dish. Drizzle with orange sauce; garnish with orange segments. **Yield:** 6 servings.

Quick TIP

You can instantly increase the flavor of white or brown rice by simmering it in low-sodium chicken broth instead of water. Similarly, stir a few teaspoons of orange juice into cooked rice, or toss in some diced nuts or dried fruit. Try adding a little soy sauce, garlic salt or onion powder to frozen veggies shortly before serving for another fast side dish.

Spinach Potatoes Au Gratin

Spinach Potatoes Au Gratin
(Pictured above)
Prep/Total Time: 30 min.

Edna Shaffer • Beulah, Michigan
This creamy mixture of sliced potatoes and spinach makes a pretty side dish. It may seem like it's labor-intensive, but it's truly not.

  5 cups thinly sliced red potatoes (about 7 large potatoes)
1/4 cup water
  3 tablespoons butter
1/4 cup chopped onion
1/4 cup all-purpose flour
  2 cups milk
  1 cup (4 ounces) shredded cheddar cheese
  1 teaspoon salt
  1 cup chopped fresh spinach
  1 tablespoon diced pimientos
  4 bacon strips, cooked and crumbled

In a 2-qt. microwave-safe dish, combine potatoes and water. Cover and microwave on high for 8-9 minutes or until potatoes are tender, stirring twice. Drain; set potatoes aside.

In a large microwave-safe bowl, heat butter on high until melted, about 30 seconds. Add onion. Microwave, uncovered, for 1-2 minutes or until tender, stirring once.

Whisk in flour until blended. Gradually stir in the milk. Cook, uncovered, on high for 2-1/2 minutes; stir. Cook 3-4 minutes longer, stirring every minute, or until sauce is thickened and bubbly. Stir in cheese and salt. Pour over potatoes. Add spinach and pimientos; mix well.

Microwave, uncovered, on high for 2-3 minutes or until heated through, stirring once. Sprinkle with bacon. **Yield:** 8 servings.

Tangy Cheese-Topped Spuds
Prep/Total Time: 20 min.

Letha Burdette • Greer, South Carolina
Horseradish provides the zing in this cheesy topping for potatoes. My family loves these vegetables that are a great way to spice up dinner on hectic nights, regardless of what the entree is.

  1 package (8 ounces) cream cheese, softened
  1 cup (8 ounces) sour cream
1/4 cup finely chopped onion
  2 tablespoons prepared horseradish
  1 to 2 tablespoons lemon juice
  2 tablespoons minced fresh parsley
1/2 teaspoon salt
  4 hot baked potatoes
1/2 cup shredded sharp cheddar cheese

In a large mixing bowl, blend cream cheese and sour cream until smooth. Add onion, horseradish, lemon juice, parsley and salt; mix well.

With a sharp knife, cut an X in the top of each potato; fluff pulp with a fork. Top with cream cheese mixture; sprinkle with cheese. **Yield:** 4 servings.

Sunny Snow Peas
Prep/Total Time: 25 min.

Kathleen Bailey • Chester Springs, Pennsylvania
Turn crispy snow peas into something special by tossing them with this lovely honey-orange sauce. I enjoy serving fresh vegetables, especially when I can prepare a sauce that seems to add the bright warmth of the sun.

1/2 cup orange juice
  2 tablespoons honey
  1 tablespoon butter
  1 to 2 teaspoons grated orange peel
1/2 teaspoon salt
1/8 teaspoon ground cardamom
  1 pound fresh snow peas *or* sugar snap peas

In a small saucepan, combine the orange juice, honey, butter, orange peel, salt and cardamom; bring to a boil. Reduce heat; simmer, uncovered, until mixture is reduced by half, about 15 minutes.

Meanwhile, in another saucepan, bring 1 in. of water and peas to a boil. Reduce heat; cover and simmer for 3-4 minutes or until crisp-tender. Drain and transfer to a serving bowl. Pour sauce over peas; toss to coat. **Yield:** 6 servings.

Bacon-Topped Brussels Sprouts

Patchwork Rice Pilaf

(Pictured below)
Prep/Total Time: 10 min.

Brenda Scarbeary • Oelwin, Iowa
Colorful, versatile and fast, this side dish always disappears at potlucks, picnics or family dinners. Even though the apples bring a subtle sweetness to the rice, the pilaf goes well with a variety of foods.

       4 celery ribs, chopped
       2 large onions, chopped
       4 medium carrots, chopped
       1 large green pepper, chopped
     1/4 cup butter, cubed
       2 medium tart red apples, chopped
       2 cups sliced fresh mushrooms
       2 packages (6.2 ounces *each*) fast-cooking long grain and wild rice mix
       2 cans (10-1/2 ounces *each*) condensed chicken broth, undiluted
 1-1/2 cups water
     1/2 cup slivered almonds

In a large skillet or saucepan, saute the celery, onions, carrots and green pepper in butter until crisp-tender. Add the apples and mushrooms; saute for 2 minutes. Stir in the rice, contents of seasoning packets, broth and water; bring to a boil. Reduce heat; cover and simmer according to rice package directions or until rice is tender and liquid is absorbed. Sprinkle with almonds. **Yield:** 12 servings.

Bacon-Topped Brussels Sprouts

(Pictured above)
Prep/Total Time: 20 min.

Lynne Howard • Annandale, Virginia
I love brussels sprouts and used to grow them in our garden when my children were small. I created this easy recipe myself, but I keep on the lookout for new ways to prepare sprouts.

       1 package (16 ounces) frozen brussels sprouts
       2 tablespoons butter, melted
     1/2 teaspoon garlic salt
     1/4 teaspoon onion powder
     1/4 teaspoon dried oregano
     1/2 pound sliced bacon, cooked and crumbled

Cook brussels sprouts according to package directions; drain. Add butter, garlic salt, onion powder and oregano; toss. Place in a serving dish. Top with bacon. **Yield:** 4-6 servings.

Quick TIP
Convenience items are a lifesaver in the side dish department. Add homemade appeal to boxed pasta and rice items by stirring in a dash of your favorite herbs or seasonings. Add a handful of frozen peas or corn kernels, or top the side dish with some slivered almonds, sunflower kernels or toasted sesame seeds. Chopped fresh parsley adds a fast spark of color.

Patchwork Rice Pilaf

Zippy Green Beans

Zippy Green Beans
(Pictured above)
Prep/Total Time: 20 min.

Suzanne McKinley • Lyons, Georgia
This homemade sweet-and-sour sauce makes fresh green beans a little bit more special. Try the tangy treatment with most any meal.

      4 cups fresh *or* frozen green beans, cut into
           2-inch pieces
      2 bacon strips, diced
      1 medium onion, thinly sliced
  1/2 cup white wine *or* apple juice
      3 tablespoons sugar
      3 tablespoons tarragon vinegar
  1/4 teaspoon salt
      2 teaspoons cornstarch
      1 tablespoon cold water

Place beans in a saucepan and cover with water; bring to a boil. Cook, uncovered, for 8-10 minutes or until crisp-tender.

Meanwhile, in a large nonstick skillet, cook bacon over medium heat until crisp. Remove with a slotted spoon to paper towels. Drain, reserving 1 teaspoon drippings. In the same skillet, saute onion until tender. Add wine or apple juice, sugar, vinegar and salt.

Combine cornstarch and cold water until smooth; add to the skillet. Bring to a boil; cook and stir for 2 minutes or until thickened. Drain beans; top with onion mixture. Sprinkle with bacon; toss to coat. **Yield:** 6 servings.

Triple-Grain Pilaf
Prep/Total Time: 30 min.

Looking for a side dish with a pleasant nutty flavor? Our Test Kitchen came up with this easy pilaf recipe that's a perfect accompaniment to poultry, beef or fish. The combination of rice, bulgur and barley gives it a nice blend of textures.

  1/2 cup sliced green onions
      1 tablespoon butter
      1 cup uncooked long grain rice
  1/2 cup bulgur
  1/2 cup quick-cooking barley
3-1/2 cups beef broth
  1/2 teaspoon salt
  1/4 teaspoon pepper
  1/4 cup chopped fresh parsley

In a large nonstick saucepan, saute onions in butter for 2 minutes. Stir in the rice, bulgur and barley; saute for 3 minutes. Add broth, salt and pepper. Bring to a boil. Reduce heat; cover and simmer for 20-25 minutes or until the rice is tender. Stir in parsley. **Yield:** 7 servings.

Editor's Note: Look for bulgur in the cereal, rice or organic food aisle of your grocery store.

Speedy Sweet Potatoes
Prep/Total Time: 15 min.

Beth Buhler • Lawrence, Kansas
I discovered this yummy sweet potato recipe years ago. There's no need for lots of butter and sugar because the pineapple and marshmallows provide plenty of sweetness. It's a holiday favorite at our house that frees up my time in the kitchen.

      2 cans (15-3/4 ounces *each*) sweet potatoes,
           drained
  1/2 teaspoon salt
      1 can (8 ounces) crushed pineapple, drained
  1/4 cup coarsely chopped pecans
      1 tablespoon brown sugar
      1 cup miniature marshmallows, *divided*
Ground nutmeg

In a 1-1/2-qt. microwave-safe dish, layer sweet potatoes, salt, pineapple, pecans, brown sugar and 1/2 cup marshmallows. Cover and microwave on high for 5-7 minutes or until bubbly around the edges. Top with the remaining marshmallows.

Microwave, uncovered, on high for 1-2 minutes or until marshmallows puff. Sprinkle with nutmeg. **Yield:** 6 servings.

Editor's Note: This recipe was tested with an 850-watt microwave.

Tomato-Garlic Angel Hair

Prep/Total Time: 15 min.

Salvatore Bertolinio • Indiana, Pennsylvania
Whether served as a side dish or an effortless main course, you're sure to enjoy this heavenly pasta dish. Feel free to add whatever ingredients your gang would appreciate most.

    1 package (1 pound) angel hair pasta
    3 large ripe tomatoes, peeled, seeded and chopped
1/3 cup olive oil
1/4 cup grated Parmesan cheese
1/4 cup minced fresh parsley
    1 to 2 garlic cloves, minced
    1 tablespoon minced fresh basil
1/4 teaspoon garlic salt

Cook pasta according to package directions. Meanwhile, in a large bowl, combine remaining ingredients. Rinse and drain pasta; add to tomato mixture and toss to coat. Serve immediately. **Yield:** 8-10 servings.

Cinnamon Carrots

(Pictured below)
Prep/Total Time: 10 min.

Charlene Kalb • Catonsville, Maryland
When my daughter was a little girl, the only vegetables she would eat were carrots covered in a packaged glaze. I ran out of glaze one day and created this no-fuss recipe. I never bought a prepared glaze again.

    1 package (16 ounces) frozen sliced carrots
1/4 cup honey
    1 to 2 tablespoons butter
1/2 to 1 teaspoon ground cinnamon

Cook carrots according to package directions. Meanwhile, in a saucepan, heat the honey, butter and cinnamon until butter is melted; stir to blend. Drain carrots; place in a serving bowl. Drizzle with honey mixture. **Yield:** 6 servings.

Cinnamon Carrots

Salsa Rice

Salsa Rice

(Pictured above)
Prep/Total Time: 15 min.

Molly Ingle • Canton, North Carolina
It's a snap to change the spice level in this popular rice side dish by choosing a milder or hotter salsa. It's a delicious way to round out burritos, tacos or enchiladas when the clock is ticking.

1-1/2 cups water
1-1/2 cups chunky salsa
    2 cups uncooked instant rice
    1 to 1-1/2 cups shredded Colby-Monterey Jack cheese

In a saucepan, bring water and salsa to a boil. Stir in rice. Remove from the heat; cover and let stand for 5 minutes. Stir in cheese; cover and let stand for 30 seconds or until cheese is melted. **Yield:** 5 servings.

Like-Homemade Baked Beans

Prep/Total Time: 25 min.

Sue Thomas • Casa Grande, Arizona
Looking for a speedy way to jazz up canned pork and beans? Try giving them homemade taste with bacon, onion, brown sugar and Worcestershire sauce. It's a real people-pleaser at backyard barbecues.

    2 bacon strips, diced
1/2 cup chopped onion
    1 can (15-3/4 ounces) pork and beans
    2 tablespoons brown sugar
1-1/2 teaspoons Worcestershire sauce
1/2 teaspoon ground mustard

In a large skillet, cook bacon until crisp. Add onion; cook until tender. Add remaining ingredients. Reduce heat; simmer for 10-15 minutes or until heated through, stirring frequently. **Yield:** 3 servings.

Spicy Orange Beef (p.46)

Chapter 5

Beef & Ground Beef

The meat-and-potatoes lovers in your home will leave the table satisfied when you whip up any of the following 24 mainstays. Best of all, each entree is ready in half an hour...or less!

Mushroom Cube Steaks

In the same skillet, saute mushrooms and onion in remaining butter until tender. Add parsley and remaining Worcestershire sauce. Return steaks to skillet; cover and simmer for 5-7 minutes or until meat is tender. **Yield:** 2 servings.

Spicy Orange Beef

(Pictured on page 44)
Prep/Total Time: 30 min.

Heather Ford • Pullman, Washington
When I first started cooking, I did a lot of stir-frying. Although my menu has expanded, I still enjoy whipping up stir-fries when the clock is ticking. Oranges, ginger and pepper flakes give this one a distinctive flavor.

  1/4 cup orange juice concentrate
    3 tablespoons soy sauce
    3 tablespoons water
    1 tablespoon cornstarch
    1 tablespoon finely grated orange peel
    1 teaspoon sugar
    5 tablespoons vegetable oil, *divided*
    2 garlic cloves, minced
    4 cups fresh broccoli florets
  12 green onions with tops, cut into 1-inch pieces
  1/2 teaspoon ground ginger
  1/4 teaspoon crushed red pepper flakes
    1 pound boneless beef sirloin steak, cut into thin strips
    3 medium oranges, sectioned
Hot cooked rice

In a small bowl, combine the first six ingredients; set aside. In a large skillet or wok, heat 3 tablespoons oil over medium heat; saute garlic for 30 seconds. Add broccoli, onions, ginger and pepper flakes; stir-fry for 2 minutes or until broccoli is crisp-tender. Remove vegetables and keep warm.

Heat remaining oil in skillet; add beef. Stir-fry until no longer pink. Stir orange juice mixture; add to skillet. Cook and stir for 2 minutes or until sauce is thickened. Return vegetables to pan. Add oranges and heat through. Serve over rice. **Yield:** 6 servings.

Mushroom Cube Steaks

(Pictured above)
Prep/Total Time: 25 min.

Marie Ritchie • Apple Valley, California
When my husband retired, we sold our home and traveled the country for 10 years in our house trailer. We tried foods we never ate before and exchanged recipes with others. This steak dish from a traveling friend is one we turn to often.

    1 tablespoon all-purpose flour
  1/4 teaspoon salt
Dash pepper
    2 beef cube steaks (1/4 to 1/3 pound *each*)
    2 tablespoons butter, *divided*
    1 teaspoon Dijon mustard
    1 teaspoon Worcestershire sauce, *divided*
  1/2 pound fresh mushrooms, sliced
    1 tablespoon chopped onion
    2 tablespoons minced fresh parsley

In a large resealable plastic bag, combine the flour, salt and pepper. Add beef, a piece at a time, and shake to coat.

In a large skillet brown steak over medium heat, in 1 tablespoon butter until meat is no long pink. Remove the steaks to a serving platter; spread each with 1/2 teaspoon mustard. Pour 1/4 teaspoon Worcestershire sauce over each; keep warm.

Quick TIP

When chopping items for a stir-fry or other skillet dish, remember that thinner or smaller pieces of beef and vegetables will cook much quicker than larger pieces of food.

Western Chili Casserole

(Pictured below)
Prep/Total Time: 25 min.

Terri Mock • American Falls, Idaho
I'm a student and my husband is a truck driver. With three children going in three different directions every day, easy yet scrumptious meals are a must in our household. This hot bake fits the bill.

> 1 pound ground beef
> 1 large onion, chopped
> 1 celery rib, chopped
> 1 can (15 ounces) chili with beans
> 1-1/2 cups corn chips, coarsely crushed, *divided*
> 3/4 cup shredded cheddar cheese

In a large skillet, cook the beef, onion and celery over medium heat until meat is no longer pink and vegetables are tender; drain. Stir in the chili and 1/2 cup of chips.

Transfer to a greased 1-1/2-qt. baking dish. Sprinkle remaining chips around edge of dish; fill center with cheese. Bake, uncovered, at 350° for 10 minutes or until heated through. **Yield:** 4 servings.

Reuben Casserole

Western Chili Casserole

Reuben Casserole

(Pictured above)
Prep/Total Time: 30 min.

Nita White • Cedar Springs, Michigan
I always get compliments when I take this wonderful, full-flavored casserole to bring-a-dish dinners. It's so satisfying and comforting, yet it doesn't require me to spend a lot of time in the kitchen.

> 1 can (14 ounces) sauerkraut, rinsed and well drained
> 1 cup Thousand Island dressing
> 1 pound thinly sliced deli corned beef, cut into strips
> 2 cups (8 ounces) shredded Swiss cheese
> 4 to 6 slices rye bread, buttered

Combine sauerkraut and salad dressing; spread into a greased 13-in. x 9-in. x 2-in. baking dish. Top with corned beef and cheese.

Place bread, buttered side up, over top. Bake, uncovered, at 375° for 25-30 minutes or until heated through and bubbly. **Yield:** 4 servings.

Steak and Vegetables

Steak and Vegetables
(Pictured above)
Prep/Total Time: 20 min.

Melanie Bowman • Midland, Texas
Soy sauce flavors this simple combination of garden-fresh veggies and tender strips of sirloin. Served over rice, it's a hearty meal-in-one.

   1 tablespoon cornstarch
   1 teaspoon reduced-sodium beef bouillon
     granules
   1 cup cold water
1/4 cup reduced-sodium soy sauce
 10 ounces boneless beef sirloin steak
   1 medium green pepper, julienned
   1 medium onion, halved and sliced
   1 garlic clove, minced
   2 teaspoons canola oil
   2 medium tomatoes, cut into eighths
   1 can (8 ounces) sliced water chestnuts,
     drained
1/8 teaspoon pepper
   4 cups hot cooked rice

In a large bowl, combine the cornstarch, bouillon, water and soy sauce; set aside. Cut steak thinly across the grain, then cut slices in half; set aside.

In a nonstick skillet or wok, stir-fry green pepper, onion and garlic in oil for 4 minutes; remove and set aside. Add meat; stir-fry for 4-6 minutes.

Stir cornstarch mixture and add to pan. Bring to a boil; cook and stir for 1 minute or until thickened. Add tomatoes, water chestnuts and green pepper mixture; cook and stir until heated through. Sprinkle with pepper. Serve over the rice. **Yield: 4 servings.**

Flip-Over Pizza
Prep/Total Time: 30 min.

Karen Duncan • Franklin, Nebraska
Your family is sure to enjoy this easy pizza that you flip over before serving. We like it in the summer when we don't want to heat up the house.

   1 pound ground beef
   1 celery rib, chopped
   1 medium onion, chopped
1/4 cup chopped green pepper
   1 can (10-1/2 ounces) pizza sauce
Salt to taste
3/4 cup biscuit/baking mix
   3 to 4 tablespoons milk
3/4 cup shredded part-skim mozzarella cheese
   2 tablespoons grated Parmesan cheese

Crumble beef into a microwave-safe 9-in. pie plate. Sprinkle with celery, onion and green pepper. Cover and microwave on high for 7 minutes or until meat is no longer pink and vegetables are tender, stirring once; drain. Stir in the pizza sauce and salt.

Combine biscuit mix and milk just until combined. Roll out on a lightly floured surface into a 9-in. circle; place over meat mixture.

Microwave, uncovered, on high for 8 minutes or until a toothpick inserted into crust comes out clean. Invert onto a serving plate. Sprinkle with cheeses. **Yield: 4 servings.**

Editor's Note: This recipe was tested with an 850-watt microwave.

Garden Skillet Supper
Prep/Total Time: 25 min.

Suzan Hatcher • Sand Springs, Oklahoma
Our family gave this stovetop dish its name because I use whichever vegetables are in season in our garden patch.

   1 cup uncooked long grain rice
   1 tablespoon olive oil
   2 garlic cloves, minced
   1 cup chopped onion
1/2 cup chopped green pepper
1/2 cup chopped sweet red pepper
   1 pound ground beef, browned and drained
   2 cups chopped seeded tomatoes

Cook rice according to package directions. In a large skillet, saute garlic, onion and peppers in oil until tender. Stir in browned beef, tomatoes and rice; cook until heated through. **Yield: 4-6 servings.**

Tamale Pie

Tamale Pie
(Pictured above)
Prep/Total Time: 30 min.

Nancy Roberts • Cave City, Arkansas
My whole gang really enjoys Mexican food. When time is tight, I make this zesty deep-dish pie. It always satisfies their appetites and keeps us on schedule.

   1 pound ground beef
1/4 pound bulk pork sausage
1/4 cup chopped onion
   1 garlic clove, minced
   1 can (14-1/2 ounces) stewed tomatoes,
     drained
   1 can (11 ounces) whole kernel corn, drained
   1 can (6 ounces) tomato paste
1/4 cup sliced ripe olives
1-1/2 teaspoons chili powder
1/2 teaspoon salt
   1 egg
1/3 cup milk
   1 package (8-1/2 ounces) corn bread/muffin
     mix
Dash paprika
1/2 cup shredded cheddar cheese

In a 2-1/2-qt. microwave-safe dish, combine beef, sausage, onion and garlic. Cover and microwave on high for 5-6 minutes, stirring once to crumble meat. Drain. Add the tomatoes, corn, tomato paste, olives, chili powder and salt; mix well. Cover and microwave on high for 6-8 minutes or until heated through.

   In a large bowl, beat egg; add milk and corn bread mix. Stir just until moistened. Spoon over meat mixture; sprinkle with paprika.

   Microwave, uncovered, on high for 10-11 minutes or until a toothpick inserted near the center of the corn bread comes out clean. Sprinkle with cheese. **Yield:** 6 servings.

Editor's Note: This recipe was tested with an 850-watt microwave.

Tangy Mini Meat Loaves
(Pictured below)
Prep/Total Time: 20 min.

Paula Martin • Paxinos, Pennsylvania
It's fun to make miniature meat loaves instead of one big loaf...and they cook up quicker in a skillet than in the oven. In fact, this two-person recipe is one of my old standbys for a speedy meal.

1/2 pound ground beef
1/2 cup sliced onion
1/4 cup dark corn syrup
   3 tablespoons steak sauce
   2 teaspoons spicy brown mustard

Shape beef into four small loaves, 1/4 to 1/2 in. thick. Cook in a skillet over medium-high heat for 3-4 minutes on each side or until no longer pink. Remove to a serving plate and keep warm.

   Drain all but 1 tablespoon drippings; saute onion in drippings until tender. Add corn syrup, steak sauce and mustard; bring to a boil. Pour over meat loaves and serve immediately. **Yield:** 2 servings.

Tangy Mini Meat Loaves

Steak Fajitas

Steak Fajitas
(Pictured above)
Prep/Total Time: 30 min.

Shirley Hilger • Lincoln, Nebraska
Juicy strips of sirloin pick up plenty of spicy flavor from this marinade seasoned with cayenne pepper and cumin. The fajitas are always a fast and satisfying answer to dinnertime.

- 1/4 cup orange juice
- 1/4 cup white vinegar
- 4 garlic cloves, minced
- 1 teaspoon seasoned salt
- 1 teaspoon dried oregano
- 1 teaspoon ground cumin
- 1/4 teaspoon cayenne pepper
- 1 pound boneless beef sirloin steak, cut into 1/4-inch strips
- 1 medium onion, thinly sliced
- 1 medium green pepper, thinly sliced
- 1 medium sweet red pepper, thinly sliced
- 2 tablespoons vegetable oil, *divided*
- 4 to 6 flour tortillas (10 inches), warmed
- Shredded cheddar cheese, picante sauce and sour cream, optional

In a large resealable plastic bag, combine the orange juice, vinegar, garlic and seasonings; add the beef. Seal bag and turn to coat; set aside. In a skillet, saute onion and peppers in 1 tablespoon oil

until crisp-tender; remove and set aside.

Drain and discard marinade. In the same skillet, cook beef in remaining oil for 2-4 minutes or until it reaches desired doneness. Return vegetables to pan; heat through. Spoon meat and vegetables onto tortillas. If desired, top with cheese and serve with picante sauce and sour cream. **Yield:** 4-6 servings.

Bacon Cheeseburger Rice
(Pictured below)
Prep/Total Time: 30 min.

Joyce Whipps • West Des Moines, Iowa
My husband and I set out to create a tasty skillet dish, and this was the result. I've had teenage nieces and nephews request the recipe after their first bite.

- 1 pound ground beef
- 1-3/4 cups water
- 2/3 cup barbecue sauce
- 1 tablespoon prepared mustard
- 2 teaspoons dried minced onion
- 1/2 teaspoon pepper
- 2 cups uncooked instant rice
- 1 cup (4 ounces) shredded cheddar cheese
- 1/3 cup chopped dill pickles
- 5 bacon strips, cooked and crumbled

In a large saucepan over medium heat, cook the beef until no longer pink; drain. Add water, barbecue sauce, mustard, onion and pepper. Bring to a boil; stir in the rice. Sprinkle with cheese. Reduce heat; cover and simmer for 5 minutes. Sprinkle with pickles and bacon. **Yield:** 4-6 servings.

Bacon Cheeseburger Rice

Simple Salisbury Steak
Prep/Total Time: 30 min.

Elouise Bonar • Hanover, Illinois
Fresh mushrooms and cream of mushroom soup create a speedy simmered sauce that covers my ground beef patties. It's great for busy families with lots of hectic weeknights.

     1 egg
 1/3 cup dry bread crumbs
     1 can (10-3/4 ounces) reduced-fat reduced-sodium condensed cream of mushroom soup, undiluted, *divided*
 1/4 cup finely chopped onion
     1 pound lean ground beef
 1/2 cup fat-free milk
 1/4 teaspoon browning sauce, optional
 1/4 teaspoon salt
1-1/2 cups sliced fresh mushrooms

In a bowl, combine the egg, bread crumbs, 1/4 cup soup and onion. Crumble the beef over mixture and mix well. Shape into six patties. In a large nonstick skillet, brown the patties on both sides; drain.

In a bowl, combine the milk, browning sauce if desired, salt and remaining soup; stir in mushrooms. Pour over patties. Reduce heat; cover and simmer for 15-20 minutes or until meat is no longer pink. **Yield:** 6 servings.

Beef and Pepper Linguine
Prep/Total Time: 30 min.

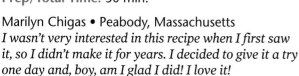

Marilyn Chigas • Peabody, Massachusetts
I wasn't very interested in this recipe when I first saw it, so I didn't make it for years. I decided to give it a try one day and, boy, am I glad I did! I love it!

 1 pound ground beef
 1 large onion, chopped
 2 medium green peppers, cubed
 1 package (16 ounces) linguine, cooked and drained
 4 to 6 tablespoons soy sauce
Dash garlic powder, optional

In a large skillet, cook beef, onion and green peppers over medium heat until meat is no longer pink; drain. Remove from the heat. Add linguine and soy sauce; mix well. Sprinkle with garlic powder if desired. **Yield:** 6 servings.

Beef Tenderloin in Mushroom Sauce

Beef Tenderloin in Mushroom Sauce
(Pictured above)
Prep/Total Time: 30 min.

Denise McNab • Warrington, Pennsylvania
It doesn't take much fuss to fix a special meal for two. Here's the delicious proof.

     1 teaspoon vegetable oil
     4 tablespoons butter, *divided*
     2 beef tenderloin steaks *or* fillets (1 inch thick)
 1/2 cup chopped fresh mushrooms
     1 tablespoon chopped green onion
     1 tablespoon all-purpose flour
 1/8 teaspoon salt
Dash pepper
 2/3 cup chicken *or* beef broth
 1/8 teaspoon browning sauce, optional

In a large skillet, heat oil and 2 tablespoons of butter over medium-high heat. Cook steaks for 6-7 minutes on each side or until meat is done as desired (for medium-rare, a meat thermometer should read 145°; medium, 160°; well-done, 170°). Remove to a serving platter; keep warm.

To pan juices, add the mushrooms, onions and remaining butter; saute until tender. Add flour, salt and pepper; gradually stir in broth until smooth. Add browning sauce if desired. Bring to a boil; boil and stir for 2 minutes. Spoon over the steaks. Serve immediately. **Yield:** 2 servings.

Pepper Steak with Squash

Pepper Steak With Squash
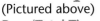
(Pictured above)
Prep/Total Time: 30 min.

Gayle Lewis • Yucaipa, California
I like to fix colorful stir-fries with savory strips of flank steak and plenty of veggies. We serve this filling dish over rice for a satisfying supper that's on the table in just 30 minutes or less.

- 1 pound beef flank steak, cut into thin strips
- 2 tablespoons vegetable oil, *divided*
- 1 medium green pepper, julienned
- 1 medium sweet red pepper, julienned
- 2 medium zucchini, julienned
- 1 small onion, cut into 1/4-inch strips
- 3 garlic cloves, minced
- 1 cup fresh *or* frozen snow peas
- 1 cup sliced fresh mushrooms
- 1 can (8 ounces) sliced water chestnuts, drained
- 3 tablespoons cornstarch
- 1 can (14-1/2 ounces) reduced-sodium beef broth
- 2 tablespoons reduced-sodium soy sauce
Hot cooked rice

In a large skillet, cook steak over medium-high heat, in 1 tablespoon oil until meat is no longer pink; drain. Remove and keep warm.

In the same skillet, saute the green and sweet red peppers in remaining oil for 2 minutes or until tender. Stir in zucchini, onion and garlic; cook and stir 2 minutes longer. Add the peas, mushrooms and water chestnuts. Saute until the vegetables are tender, about 2 minutes.

Return beef to the skillet. Combine cornstarch, broth and soy sauce until smooth; add to skillet. Bring to a boil; cook and stir for 2 minutes or until thickened. Serve over rice. **Yield:** 6 servings.

Country-Fried Steak
(Pictured below)
Prep/Total Time: 20 min.

Betty Claycomb • Alverton, Pennsylvania
This down-home main course is simple to make and so delicious! No one suspects that it comes together in less than half an hour.

- 3/4 cup buttermilk
- 1 cup crushed saltines
- 1/2 cup all-purpose flour
- 1/2 teaspoon salt
- 1/2 teaspoon pepper
- 4 beef cube steaks (1 pound)
- 3 tablespoons vegetable oil
- 1 can (10-3/4 ounces) condensed cream of mushroom soup, undiluted
- 1 cup milk

Place buttermilk and cracker crumbs in separate shallow bowls. In another shallow bowl, combine flour, salt and pepper. Coat beef with flour mixture, then dip in milk and roll in crumbs.

In a large skillet over medium-high heat, cook steaks in oil for 2-3 minutes on each side or until golden and no longer pink. Remove and keep warm. Add soup and milk to skillet; bring to a boil, stirring to loosen browned bits from pan. Serve gravy with steaks. **Yield:** 4 servings.

Country-Fried Steak

Stovetop Chili Casserole
Prep/Total Time: 25 min.

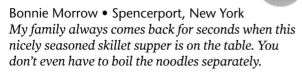

Rhonda Hogan • Eugene, Oregon
Loaded with beans, tomatoes, onion and noodles, there's plenty to enjoy in this no-stress dish. Serve it with corn bread for a great supper.

- 1 pound ground beef
- 1/2 cup chopped onion
- 1 can (16 ounces) kidney beans, rinsed and drained
- 1 can (15 ounces) tomato sauce
- 1 can (14-1/2 ounces) stewed tomatoes
- 1/4 teaspoon garlic powder
- 1/4 teaspoon salt
- 1/4 teaspoon pepper
- 2 cups cooked noodles

In a large skillet, cook beef and onion over medium heat until beef is no longer pink; drain. Stir in the beans, tomato sauce, tomatoes, garlic powder, salt and pepper. Cover and simmer for 5 minutes. Stir in noodles; heat through. **Yield:** 6 servings.

One-Pot Dinner
Prep/Total Time: 30 min.

Bonnie Morrow • Spencerport, New York
My family always comes back for seconds when this nicely seasoned skillet supper is on the table. You don't even have to boil the noodles separately.

- 1/2 pound ground beef
- 1 medium onion, chopped
- 1 cup chopped celery
- 3/4 cup chopped green pepper
- 2 teaspoons Worcestershire sauce
- 1 teaspoon salt, optional
- 1/2 teaspoon dried basil
- 1/4 teaspoon pepper
- 2 cups uncooked medium egg noodles
- 1 can (16 ounces) kidney beans, rinsed and drained
- 1 can (14-1/2 ounces) stewed tomatoes
- 3/4 cup water
- 1 beef bouillon cube

In a large saucepan or skillet, cook meat until no longer pink; drain. Add onion, celery and green pepper; cook for 5 minutes or until vegetables are crisp-tender. Add Worcestershire sauce, salt if desired, basil and pepper.

Stir in noodles, beans, tomatoes, water and bouillon. Bring to a boil. Reduce heat; cover and simmer for 20 minutes or until noodles are tender, stirring occasionally. **Yield:** 5 servings.

Greek-Style Rib Eye Steaks

Greek-Style Rib Eye Steaks
(Pictured above)
Prep/Total Time: 25 min.

Ruby Williams • Bogalusa, Louisiana
Because our children are grown, I often cook for just my husband and me. When I want to serve something special, this is the entree I usually reach for. Seasonings, black olives and feta cheese give the steak such great flavor. Best of all, it's one main course that I can set on the table in under 30 minutes.

- 1-1/2 teaspoons garlic powder
- 1-1/2 teaspoons dried oregano
- 1-1/2 teaspoons dried basil
- 1/2 teaspoon salt
- 1/8 teaspoon pepper
- 2 boneless beef rib eye steaks (1-1/2 inches thick and 8 ounces *each*)
- 1 tablespoon olive oil
- 1 tablespoon lemon juice
- 2 tablespoons crumbled feta cheese
- 1 tablespoon sliced ripe olives

In a small bowl, combine the first five ingredients; rub onto both sides of steaks.

In a large skillet, cook steaks in oil for 7-9 minutes on each side or until meat reaches desired doneness (for medium-rare a meat thermometer should read 145°, medium, 160°, well-done, 170°). Sprinkle with lemon juice, cheese and olives. Serve immediately. **Yield:** 2 servings.

Stir-Fried Steak and Veggies

Stir-Fried Steak And Veggies
(Pictured above)
Prep/Total Time: 20 min.

Inez Glover • Wainwright, Alberta
There's just enough ginger, chili powder and garlic powder in the sauce to spark the flavor of this swift dinner. For variety, substitute chicken or pork for the sirloin. If I'm in a hurry or don't have fresh vegetables on hand, I'll reach for two bags of frozen stir-fry vegetables instead.

    1 tablespoon cornstarch
    1 tablespoon brown sugar
  3/4 teaspoon ground ginger
  1/2 teaspoon chili powder
  1/4 teaspoon garlic powder
  1/4 teaspoon pepper
  1/2 cup cold water
  1/4 cup soy sauce
    1 pound boneless sirloin steak, cut into thin strips
    2 tablespoons vegetable oil
    2 cups broccoli florets
    2 cups cauliflowerets
    1 large onion, chopped
    1 cup sliced carrots
Hot cooked rice

In a small bowl, whisk together the first eight ingredients until smooth; set aside.

In a skillet or wok, stir-fry steak in oil for 3-5 minutes. Add broccoli, cauliflower, onion, carrots and soy sauce mixture; cover and cook for 8 minutes or until vegetables are crisp-tender, stirring occasionally. Serve over rice. **Yield:** 4 servings.

Beef Skillet Supper
Prep/Total Time: 30 min.

Tabitha Allen • Cypress, Texas
Topped with cheese and featuring canned Mexicorn, this one-dish entree offers lots of flavor and convenience. Best of all, it's ready in no time.

    1 package (8 ounces) medium egg noodles
1-1/2 pounds ground beef
    1 medium onion, chopped
    1 can (8 ounces) tomato sauce
  1/2 cup water
    1 can (11 ounces) Mexicorn, drained
  1/2 teaspoon salt
  1/4 teaspoon pepper
    1 cup (4 ounces) shredded cheddar cheese

Cook noodles according to package directions. Meanwhile, in a skillet, cook beef and onion over medium heat until meat is no longer pink; drain. Add the tomato sauce and water. Cover and cook for 8 minutes.

Drain the noodles; add to beef mixture. Add corn, salt and pepper. Sprinkle with cheese; cover and cook until heated through and the cheese is melted. **Yield:** 8-10 servings.

Meat Loaf Pattie
Prep/Total Time: 15 min.

Dorothy Hunt • Waltham, Massachusetts
With this recipe, we can have a hearty meat loaf dinner without dealing with lots of leftovers and without a lot of work. That delights both my husband and me.

  1/3 cup seasoned bread crumbs
    3 tablespoons milk
    1 teaspoon Worcestershire sauce
    1 teaspoon finely chopped onion
  1/4 teaspoon salt
  1/2 pound lean ground beef
Ketchup

In a bowl, combine the first five ingredients. Crumble beef over mixture and mix well. Shape into a large pattie.

Place in a shallow microwave-safe dish. Microwave, uncovered, on high for 3-4 minutes or until a meat thermometer reads 160°. Let stand for 3 minutes. Serve with ketchup. **Yield:** 2 servings.

Editor's Note: This recipe was tested with an 850-watt microwave. The meat loaf may also be baked at 350° for 20 minutes or until a meat thermometer reads 160°.

Dressed-Up Meatballs

(Pictured below)

Prep/Total Time: 20 min.

Ivy Eresmas • Dade City, Florida

Frozen meatballs and a jar of sweet-and-sour sauce make this meal a lifesaver when racing against the clock. The flavorful sauce is dressed up with a hint of garlic and nicely coats the mixture of meatballs, carrots, green pepper and onion.

        2 pounds frozen fully cooked meatballs,
          thawed
        1 small onion, sliced
        2 medium carrots, julienned
        1 small green pepper, julienned
        1 garlic clove, minced
        1 jar (10 ounces) sweet-and-sour sauce
    4-1/2 teaspoons soy sauce
    Hot cooked rice

Place the meatballs in a 3-qt. microwave-safe dish; top with the onion, carrots, green pepper and garlic. Combine the sauces; pour over meatballs.

Cover and microwave on high for 8-10 minutes or until vegetables are tender and meatballs are heated through, stirring twice. Serve over rice. **Yield:** 8 servings.

Editor's Note: This recipe was tested with an 850-watt microwave.

Peppered Rib Eye Steaks

Peppered Rib Eye Steaks

(Pictured above)

Prep/Total Time: 20 min.

Julee Wallberg • Reno, Nevada

A wonderful assortment of herbs and seasonings flavors these juicy steaks. Prepared on the grill, they're a hit any time I serve them.

        2 tablespoons vegetable oil
      1/2 teaspoon paprika
      1/2 teaspoon pepper
      1/4 teaspoon *each* salt, garlic powder and
          lemon-pepper seasoning
      1/8 teaspoon *each* dried oregano, crushed red
          pepper flakes, ground cumin and cayenne
          pepper
        4 boneless beef rib eye steaks (about 10
          ounces *each* and 1 inch thick)

In a large bowl, combine the oil and seasonings; brush over steaks. Grill steaks, covered, over medium heat or broil 3-4 in. from the heat for 7-10 minutes on each side or until meat reaches desired doneness (for medium-rare, a meat thermometer should read 145°; medium, 160°; well-done, 170°). Baste occasionally with seasoning mixture. Let stand 3-5 minutes before serving. **Yield:** 4 servings.

Dressed-Up Meatballs

Rosemary-Garlic Chicken and Veggies (p. 58)

Chapter 6

Chicken & Turkey

Family cooks know that when it comes to fixing a fast supper, poultry is a natural fit. When you need a quick fix, consider these chicken and turkey dishes...16 of which are meal-in-one wonders.

Parmesan Chicken

Spoon over chicken; sprinkle with mozzarella cheese and remaining Parmesan cheese. Serve with pasta. **Yield:** 4 servings.

Rosemary-Garlic Chicken and Veggies

(Pictured on Page 56)
Prep/Total Time: 30 min.

Robert Dessell • Pensacola, Florida
I enjoy cooking, and this has become a signature of mine. My wife asks me to make it at least once a week. It's a simple dish to prepare.

    1/2 cup chopped sweet yellow pepper
    1/2 cup chopped sweet red pepper
      1 small onion, cut into wedges
      1 small zucchini, halved and cut into
           1/2-inch slices
      2 tablespoons olive oil, *divided*
      2 boneless skinless chicken breast halves
           (4 ounces *each*)
      2 garlic cloves, sliced
      2 fresh rosemary sprigs

Place the peppers, onion and zucchini in a greased 1-qt. baking dish; drizzle with 1 tablespoon oil and toss to coat.

In a large skillet, brown chicken in remaining oil; place over vegetables. Top with garlic and rosemary. Bake, uncovered, at 400° for 20-25 minutes or until meat juices run clear. **Yield:** 2 servings.

Parmesan Chicken

(Pictured above)
Prep/Total Time: 20 min.

Margie Eddy • Anne Arbor, Michigan
I like to make this yummy recipe when I have extra spaghetti sauce on hand. The herbed coating on the tender chicken turns nice and golden in no time.

    1/2 cup seasoned bread crumbs
    1/2 cup grated Parmesan cheese, *divided*
  1-1/2 teaspoons dried oregano, *divided*
    1/2 teaspoon dried basil
    1/2 teaspoon salt
    1/4 teaspoon pepper
      1 egg
      1 tablespoon water
      4 boneless skinless chicken breast halves
           (4 ounces *each*)
      2 tablespoons butter
      2 cups meatless spaghetti sauce
    1/2 teaspoon garlic salt
      1 cup (4 ounces) shredded part-skim
           mozzarella cheese
Hot cooked fettuccine *or* pasta of your choice

In a shallow bowl, combine the bread crumbs, 1/4 cup Parmesan cheese, 1 teaspoon oregano, basil, salt and pepper. In another shallow bowl, combine the egg and water. Dip chicken in egg mixture, then coat with crumb mixture.

In a large skillet, cook chicken in butter on both sides until juices run clear.

Meanwhile, in a large saucepan, combine the spaghetti sauce, garlic salt and remaining oregano. Cook over medium heat until heated through.

Turkey Minute Steaks
Prep/Total Time: 25 min.

Barbara Powell • Laramie, Wyoming
For a no-fuss way to dress up turkey, consider this speedy idea. You only need a handful of ingredients, most of which are kitchen staples.

    3/4 cup Italian-seasoned bread crumbs
    1/4 cup grated Parmesan cheese
    1/2 teaspoon dried basil
Salt and pepper to taste
      1 egg, beaten
  1-1/2 pounds uncooked sliced turkey breast
      3 tablespoons butter

In a shallow bowl, combine the bread crumbs, Parmesan cheese, basil, salt and pepper. In another shallow bowl, add egg. Dip turkey in egg, then in crumbs, coating both sides. Melt butter in a large skillet over medium-high heat. Cook turkey for 2-3 minutes on each side or until golden brown and juices run clear. **Yield:** 6-8 servings.

Spicy Chicken And Peppers

(Pictured below)
Prep/Total Time: 25 min.

Ruth Ann Toppins • Huntington, West Virginia
My husband didn't think he could eat chicken prepared any way but fried until he was coaxed into trying this zesty combination. Chili powder gives the skillet dish a flavorful little kick.

> 1 pound boneless skinless chicken breasts, cut into 1-inch strips
> 1-1/2 cups julienned green peppers
> 1 cup chopped onion
> 2 garlic cloves, minced
> 1 tablespoon olive oil
> 1 can (15 ounces) tomato sauce
> 1 can (14-1/2 ounces) diced tomatoes, drained
> 2 teaspoons Italian seasoning
> 1-1/2 teaspoons sugar
> 1-1/2 teaspoons chili powder
> 1/4 teaspoon salt
> 1/4 teaspoon pepper
> 4 cups cooked yolk-free noodles

Fresh parsley

In a nonstick skillet, cook the chicken, green peppers, onion and garlic in oil until chicken juices run clear. Stir in the tomato sauce, tomatoes and seasonings. Bring to a boil. Reduce heat; cook, uncovered, for 5 minutes or until thickened. Serve over noodles. Sprinkle with parsley. **Yield:** 4 servings.

Spicy Chicken and Peppers

Grilled Chicken over Spinach

Grilled Chicken Over Spinach

(Pictured above)
Prep/Total Time: 25 min.

Michelle Krzmarzick • Redondo Beach, California
With two young children to keep me busy, it's essential to have a few "ready-in-minutes" menus. Here's a recipe I've pieced together and added my own touches to. It really satisfies my family without taking up too much of my time.

> 1 to 2 tablespoons olive oil
> 1 tablespoon cider vinegar
> 1 garlic clove, minced
> 1 teaspoon dried thyme
> 1/2 teaspoon dried oregano
> 1/2 teaspoon cayenne pepper
> 1/4 teaspoon salt

Dash pepper
> 4 boneless skinless chicken breast halves (1 pound)

SAUTEED SPINACH:
> 1 green onion, finely chopped
> 1 to 2 garlic cloves, minced
> 1 to 2 tablespoons olive oil
> 1/2 pound fresh mushrooms, sliced
> 1 package (10 ounces) fresh spinach, torn

In a large bowl, combine the first eight ingredients. Spoon over chicken. Grill, uncovered, over medium heat for 7 minutes on each side or until juices run clear.

In a large skillet, saute onion and garlic in oil for 1 minute or until crisp-tender. Stir in mushrooms; saute for 3-4 minutes or until tender. Add spinach; saute for 2 minutes or until wilted. Transfer to a serving platter; top with chicken. **Yield:** 4 servings.

Turkey Stir-Fry

Turkey Stir-Fry

(Pictured above)
Prep/Total Time: 30 min.

Jackie Hannahs • Cadillac, Michigan
Ginger gives this swift stir-fry its special flavor. It's easy to prepare and even quicker when I use leftover cooked turkey.

    1 pound boneless skinless turkey breast,
      cut into 1/4-inch strips
    2 tablespoons olive oil, *divided*
    1 medium sweet red pepper, sliced
    1 cup fresh broccoli florets
  1/2 cup chopped onion
    1 garlic clove, minced
  1/4 teaspoon ground ginger
    2 teaspoons cornstarch
  1/2 cup reduced-sodium chicken broth
  1/4 cup white wine *or* additional
      reduced-sodium chicken broth
    2 tablespoons reduced-sodium soy sauce
    1 can (8 ounces) sliced water chestnuts,
      drained
  1/4 teaspoon salt-free seasoning blend
    5 cups hot cooked rice

In a large nonstick skillet or wok, stir-fry turkey in 1 tablespoon oil until no longer pink. Remove and keep warm. Stir-fry the red pepper, broccoli, onion, garlic and ginger in remaining oil for 3-4 minutes or until broccoli is crisp-tender.

In a small bowl, combine cornstarch, broth and soy sauce until smooth; stir into skillet. Bring to a boil; cook and stir for 1-2 minutes or until thickened. Add turkey, water chestnuts and seasoning blend; heat through. Serve over rice. **Yield:** 5 servings.

Chicken with Mushroom Sauce

(Pictured below)
Prep/Total Time: 30 min.

Virginia Conley • Wauwatosa, Wisconsin
A thick and creamy wine sauce makes it hard to believe this hot bake comes together in just 30 minutes. It's comfort food at its best!

    4 boneless skinless chicken breast halves
      (4 ounces *each*)
    2 tablespoons butter
    1 can (10-3/4 ounces) condensed cream of
      mushroom soup, undiluted
    1 cup (8 ounces) sour cream
    1 can (4 ounces) mushroom stems and
      pieces, drained
  1/4 cup white wine *or* chicken broth
  1/2 teaspoon garlic powder
  1/2 teaspoon salt
  1/2 teaspoon pepper
Hot cooked noodles *or* rice
Sliced almonds, toasted, optional

In a large skillet, brown chicken on both sides in butter; drain. Place in a greased 11-in. x 7-in. x 2-in. baking dish.

In a large bowl, combine the soup, sour cream, mushrooms, wine or broth, garlic powder, salt and pepper; pour over the chicken.

Bake, uncovered, at 375° for 20 minutes or until meat juices run clear. Serve chicken and sauce over noodles or rice. Sprinkle with almonds if desired. **Yield:** 4 servings.

Chicken with Mushroom Sauce

Oregano Turkey Casserole

Prep/Total Time: 30 min.

Edie DeSpain • Logan, Utah
This down-home casserole is a great way to use up extra turkey and get dinner on the table in moments. The oregano really enhances its flavor.

- 4 ounces uncooked spaghetti
- 2 cups sliced fresh mushrooms
- 1/2 cup julienned green pepper
- 1/4 cup butter, cubed
- 2 tablespoons all-purpose flour
- 2 tablespoons minced fresh oregano *or*
- 2 teaspoons dried oregano
- 1/2 teaspoon salt
- 1/4 teaspoon pepper
- 1 teaspoon chicken bouillon granules
- 1/4 cup boiling water
- 1-1/3 cups evaporated milk
- 2-1/2 cups cubed cooked turkey
- 2 tablespoons chopped pimientos
- 2 tablespoons grated Parmesan cheese

Cook spaghetti according to package directions. Meanwhile, in a large skillet, saute mushrooms and green pepper in butter until tender. Stir in flour, oregano, salt and pepper. Dissolve bouillon in water; gradually add to skillet. Stir in milk. Bring to a boil; cook and stir for 2 minutes or until thickened. Add turkey and pimientos.

Drain spaghetti; toss with the turkey mixture. Pour into a greased 11-in. x 7-in. x 2-in. baking dish. Sprinkle with Parmesan cheese. Bake, uncovered, at 350° for 18-22 minutes or until heated through. **Yield:** 6-8 servings.

Southern Fried Chicken

Prep/Total Time: 25 min.

Patricia Gowen • Amherst, Virginia
When I discovered at the last minute that I didn't have enough flour for coating the chicken I was preparing one night, I used pancake mix instead. Everyone adored the change-of-pace flavor.

- 1 cup pancake mix
- 2 to 3 teaspoons salt
- 1/4 teaspoon pepper
- 1/4 teaspoon paprika
- 1 broiler/fryer chicken (3 to 4 pounds), cut up

Oil for deep-fat frying

In a large resealable plastic bag, combine the pancake mix, salt, pepper and paprika. Add chicken, a few pieces at a time; shake to coat.

Heat 2 in. of oil in an electric skillet or deep-fat fryer to 375°. Fry chicken, a few pieces at a time for 6 minutes on each side or until golden brown and juices run clear. **Yield:** 4-6 servings.

Chicken with Fruit Stuffing

Chicken with Fruit Stuffing

(Pictured above)
Prep/Total Time: 25 min.

Theresa Stewart • New Oxford, Pennsylvania
This is my favorite kind of recipe...something that tastes so good, yet requires a minimum of preparation. The stuffing is made right in the skillet with the chicken! The half-hour dish is just right, now that my husband and I are empty nesters.

- 1 can (15-1/4 ounces) sliced peaches
- 4 boneless skinless chicken breast halves (4 ounces *each*)
- 2 tablespoons vegetable oil
- 2 tablespoons butter
- 1 tablespoon brown sugar
- 1 tablespoon cider vinegar
- 1/8 teaspoon ground allspice
- 3 cups instant chicken-flavored stuffing mix

Drain peaches, reserving juice; set the peaches aside. Add enough water to juice to measure 1 cup; set aside.

In a large skillet, brown chicken on both sides in oil. Gradually stir in the peach juice mixture, butter, brown sugar, vinegar and allspice. Bring to a boil. Reduce heat; cover and simmer for 5 minutes or until chicken juices run clear.

Stir in stuffing mix and peaches. Cover and remove from the heat. Let stand for 5 minutes or until liquid is absorbed. **Yield:** 4 servings.

Grilled Chicken With Peach Sauce

(Pictured below)
Prep/Total Time: 30 min.

Beverly Minton • Milan, Michigan
I've been cooking since I was a young girl growing up on a farm in Indiana. I've served this dish many times to family and friends, and folks always like it.

1 cup sugar
2 tablespoons cornstarch
1 cup water
2 tablespoons peach *or* orange gelatin
1 medium fresh peach, peeled and finely chopped
4 boneless skinless chicken breast halves (4 ounces *each*)

In a small saucepan, combine sugar, cornstarch and water until smooth. Bring to a boil over medium heat; cook and stir for 2 minutes. Remove from heat. Stir in gelatin powder and peach; mix well until gelatin powder is dissolved. Set aside 1 cup for serving.

Grill chicken, uncovered, over medium heat for 3 minutes on each side. Baste with some of the remaining peach sauce. Continue grilling for 6-8 minutes or until meat juices run clear, basting and turning several times. Serve with the reserved peach sauce. **Yield:** 4 servings.

Grilled Chicken with Peach Sauce

Spanish Rice With Turkey

Prep/Total Time: 30 min.

Sylvia Wallace • Adams, New York
Not everyone in the family cared for Spanish rice until they tried my main course version. Now instead of complaints, I hear, "More, please."

1 pound ground turkey breast
1/2 cup chopped onion
1/2 cup chopped green pepper
1/2 teaspoon garlic powder
2 cans (14-1/2 ounces *each*) diced tomatoes, undrained
2 cups cooked long grain brown rice
1 teaspoon sugar
1 teaspoon chili powder
1/4 teaspoon pepper
1/8 teaspoon hot pepper sauce
1/2 cup shredded reduced-fat cheddar cheese

In a large skillet, cook the turkey, onion, green pepper and garlic powder over medium heat until meat is no longer pink; drain. Stir in the next six ingredients. Bring to a boil. Reduce heat; cover and simmer for 15-20 minutes or until heated through. Sprinkle with cheese. **Yield:** 5 servings.

Chicken Alfredo

Prep/Total Time: 15 min.

Jody Stewart • Goldsboro, North Carolina
Bright broccoli, zucchini and sweet red pepper lend fresh taste to this fast chicken and pasta dish. Cream cheese makes the rich sauce a snap to stir up.

1 package (8 ounces) cream cheese, cubed
6 tablespoons butter, cubed
1/2 cup milk
1/2 teaspoon garlic powder
Salt and pepper to taste
2 boneless skinless chicken breast halves, cooked and cubed (about 1-1/2 cups)
2 cups frozen chopped broccoli, thawed
2 small zucchini, julienned
1/2 cup julienned sweet red pepper
6 ounces cooked fettuccine

In a large skillet over low heat, melt cream cheese and butter; stir until smooth. Add milk, garlic powder, salt and pepper. Cook and stir for 3 minutes or until thickened. Add chicken, broccoli, zucchini and red pepper. Cook over medium heat for 3 minutes. Reduce heat; cover and cook 5 minutes longer or until vegetables are tender. Serve over fettuccine. **Yield:** 4-6 servings.

Chicken Bean Casserole

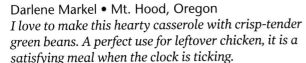

(Pictured above)
Prep/Total Time: 30 min.

Darlene Markel • Mt. Hood, Oregon
I love to make this hearty casserole with crisp-tender green beans. A perfect use for leftover chicken, it is a satisfying meal when the clock is ticking.

        6 tablespoons butter, cubed
        6 tablespoons all-purpose flour
  1-1/2 cups chicken broth
    1/2 cup milk
        1 to 2 teaspoons soy sauce
    1/2 teaspoon salt
  Dash pepper
    2/3 cup shredded Parmesan cheese, *divided*
        8 cups cut fresh green *or* wax beans, cooked
           and drained
        2 cups cubed cooked chicken

In a large saucepan, melt butter. Stir in flour until smooth. Gradually add broth, milk, soy sauce, salt and pepper. Bring to a boil; cook and stir for 2 minutes or until thickened. Remove from heat.

Stir in 1/3 cup Parmesan cheese until melted. Add beans and chicken; toss to coat.

Transfer to a greased 2-qt. baking dish; sprinkle with the remaining cheese. Bake, uncovered, at 375° for 15-18 minutes or until golden brown. **Yield:** 6-8 servings.

Chicken Bean Casserole

Almond Bacon Chicken

Almond Bacon Chicken

(Pictured above)
Prep/Total Time: 30 min.

Ruth Peterson • Jenison, Michigan
We enjoyed this flavorful dish at a friend's house years ago, and I had to have the recipe. It so quick to assemble, and it cooks in no time.

        4 bacon strips
        4 boneless skinless chicken breast halves
           (4 ounces *each*)
    1/4 teaspoon pepper
        1 can (10-3/4 ounces) condensed cream of
           onion soup, undiluted
    1/4 cup chicken broth
    1/4 cup sliced almonds, toasted

In a microwave, cook bacon on paper towels on high for 1-3 minutes or until partially cooked.

Wrap a bacon strip around each chicken breast. Sprinkle with pepper. Arrange in an 8-in. square microwave-safe dish. Cover and microwave on high for 7 minutes; drain.

In a large bowl, combine soup and broth; cover and microwave for 2 minutes. Spoon around chicken. Cook, uncovered, 5-7 minutes longer or until juices run clear. Let stand for 5 minutes before serving. Sprinkle with almonds. **Yield:** 4 servings.

Editor's Note: This recipe was tested with an 850-watt microwave.

Quick TIP If microwave cooking with a large dish, arrange the food around the edge of the platter so it cooks faster.

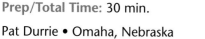
Crab-Stuffed Chicken

Cover and microwave on high for 3 minutes. Turn the chicken; sprinkle with reserved crumb mixture. Cover and cook for 2-3 minutes.

Top with spaghetti sauce. Cover and microwave on high for 5 minutes or until heated through. Sprinkle with cheese; heat, uncovered, for 1-1/2 minutes or until the cheese is melted. Let stand for 5 minutes. Serve over pasta if desired. **Yield:** 4 servings.

Nutty Turkey Slices
Prep/Total Time: 20 min.

Nancy Schmidt • Center, Colorado
Here's a fast and flavorful way to dress up turkey breast slices. You can really taste the walnuts in the crunchy golden coating. The no-fuss citrus sauce adds a delicious touch.

> 3/4 cup ground walnuts
> 1/4 cup grated Parmesan cheese
> 1/2 teaspoon Italian seasoning
> 1/2 teaspoon paprika
> 6 turkey breast slices (about 2-1/2 ounces each)
> 3 tablespoons butter
> 1 teaspoon cornstarch
> 1/2 cup chicken broth
> 2 teaspoons lemon juice

In a large resealable plastic bag, combine the walnuts, Parmesan cheese, Italian seasoning and paprika. Add chicken, a few pieces at a time, and shake to coat.

In a large skillet over medium heat, brown half of the turkey at a time in butter for 3-4 minutes on each side or until juices run clear; remove and keep warm.

Combine cornstarch, broth and lemon juice until smooth; gradually add to the skillet. Stir to loosen browned bits and bring to a boil; cook and stir for 1 minute or until thickened. Serve with turkey slices. **Yield:** 3-6 servings.

Crab-Stuffed Chicken
(Pictured above)
Prep/Total Time: 30 min.

DISH MEAL 1

Pat Durrie • Omaha, Nebraska
This is a luscious change from plain chicken. The combination of crab, chicken, spaghetti sauce and cheese is popular in my house! Serve it to guests and they'll think you fussed.

> 4 boneless skinless chicken breast halves
> 1 pouch (3.53 ounces) premium crabmeat, drained
> 1/2 cup dry bread crumbs
> 1/4 cup grated Parmesan cheese
> 1 teaspoon garlic powder
> 1 teaspoon onion powder
> 1 teaspoon dried basil
> 2 cups meatless spaghetti sauce
> 1/2 cup shredded part-skim mozzarella cheese
> Hot cooked pasta, optional

Flatten chicken to 1/4-in. thickness; top with crab. Roll up tightly and secure with toothpicks. In a shallow bowl, combine the bread crumbs, Parmesan cheese, garlic powder, onion powder and basil. Roll chicken in crumb mixture; set remaining mixture aside.

Place chicken in a shallow 1-1/2-qt. microwave-safe dish coated with nonstick cooking spray.

Quick TIP Save time by grilling several chicken breasts at once and storing them in the freezer. You'll be amazed at how often the cooked chicken comes in handy, and the charbroiled flavor is a great change of pace in winter.

Tender Lemon Chicken

(Pictured below)
Prep/Total Time: 30 min.

Lee Bremson • Kansas City, Missouri
You'll love the zesty flavor of this moist, delicious bone-in chicken entree. Using the pressure cooker cuts the cooking time in half compared to cooking the same chicken breasts in the oven.

>   1 medium onion, chopped
>   4 garlic cloves, minced
>   1 to 3 tablespoons olive oil
>   4 bone-in chicken breast halves, skin removed
>   1 cup chicken broth
> 1/4 cup water
> 1/4 cup lemon juice
> 3/4 cup minced fresh parsley
> 1/2 cup chopped celery with leaves
> 1-1/2 teaspoons Italian seasoning
> 1/2 teaspoon salt, optional
> 1/4 teaspoon pepper
> 4-1/2 teaspoons cornstarch
>   3 tablespoons cold water

In a pressure cooker, saute onion and garlic in oil until tender; remove with a slotted spoon and set aside.

Brown the chicken, a few pieces at time, in the cooker. Return onion mixture and all chicken to pan. Add broth, water, lemon juice, parsley, celery, Italian seasoning, salt if desired and pepper. Close cover securely; place pressure regulator on vent pipe.

Bring cooker to full pressure over high heat. Reduce heat to medium-high and cook for 8 minutes. (Pressure regulator should maintain a slow steady rocking motion; adjust heat if needed.)

Tender Lemon Chicken

Deluxe Turkey Club Pizza

Immediately cool according to manufacturer's directions until pressure is completely reduced. Remove chicken and keep warm.

Measure pan juice; return 1-1/2 cups to pan. Combine cornstarch and cold water until smooth; stir into pan juices. Bring to a boil; cook and stir for 2 minutes or until thickened. Serve over chicken. **Yield:** 4 servings.

Deluxe Turkey Club Pizza

(Pictured above)
Prep/Total Time: 30 min.

Philis Bukovcik • Lansing, Michigan
This unique pizza has become my family's favorite. In winter, we often stay home on Saturday nights to rent movies and indulge in its generous slices.

>   1 tube (10 ounces) refrigerated pizza crust
>   1 tablespoon sesame seeds
> 1/4 cup mayonnaise
>   1 teaspoon grated lemon peel
>   1 medium tomato, thinly sliced
> 1/2 cup cubed cooked turkey
>   4 bacon strips, cooked and crumbled
>   2 medium fresh mushrooms, thinly sliced
> 1/4 cup chopped onion
> 1-1/2 cups (6 ounces) shredded Colby-Monterey Jack cheese

Unroll pizza dough and press onto a greased 12-in. pizza pan; build up edges slightly. Sprinkle with sesame seeds. Bake at 425° for 12-14 minutes or until edges are lightly browned.

Combine mayonnaise and lemon peel; spread over crust. Top with tomato, turkey, bacon, mushrooms, onion and cheese. Bake for 6-8 minutes or until cheese is melted. Cut into slices. **Yield:** 8 slices.

Chicken with Spicy Fruit

(Pictured below)
Prep/Total Time: 30 min.

Kathy Rairigh • Milford, Indiana
This speedy stovetop entree is special enough to serve on weekends, yet easy enough for work nights. The moist chicken gets wonderful flavor from a sauce made with strawberry jam, dried cranberries and pineapple juice. I like it alongside rice pilaf, peas, a garden salad and cloverleaf rolls.

    1-1/4 cups unsweetened pineapple juice
      1/4 cup dried cranberries
        2 garlic cloves, minced
      1/8 to 1/4 teaspoon crushed red pepper flakes
        4 boneless skinless chicken breast halves
           (1 pound)
      1/4 cup strawberry spreadable fruit
        1 teaspoon cornstarch
        2 green onions, thinly sliced

In a large skillet, combine pineapple juice, cranberries, garlic and red pepper flakes; bring to a boil. Add chicken. Reduce heat; cover and simmer for 10 minutes or until chicken juices run clear. Remove chicken to a platter and keep warm.

Bring cooking liquid to a boil; cook for 5-7 minutes or until liquid is reduced to 3/4 cup. Combine spreadable fruit and cornstarch until blended; add to the skillet. Boil and stir for 1 minute or until thickened. Spoon over chicken. Sprinkle with onions. **Yield:** 4 servings.

Chicken with Spicy Fruit

Sweet-Sour Chicken Nuggets

Sweet-Sour Chicken Nuggets

(Pictured above)
Prep/Total Time: 30 min.

Arlene Best • East Ridge, Tennessee
Everyone in our family loves this meal, particularly our grandchildren. Frozen breaded chicken and canned pineapple make this dish a snap to prepare, and its sweet-tangy taste keeps them asking for more.

        1 medium green pepper, cut into chunks
        1 large onion, cut into wedges
        1 to 2 tablespoons canola oil
        1 can (14-1/2 ounces) chicken broth
      1/2 cup pancake syrup
      1/4 cup cider vinegar
        1 tablespoon soy sauce
        1 can (8 ounces) pineapple chunks
        2 to 3 tablespoons cornstarch
       20 pieces breaded chicken nuggets, thawed
Hot cooked rice

In a large skillet, saute green pepper and onion in oil until crisp-tender; remove and keep warm. Add the broth, syrup, vinegar and soy sauce to the skillet; bring to a boil.

Drain pineapple, reserving juice; set pineapple aside. Combine cornstarch and juice until smooth; gradually add to broth mixture. Bring to a boil; cook and stir for 2 minutes or until thickened.

Add chicken nuggets; cook for 2 minutes. Stir in the pineapple and sauteed vegetables; heat through. Serve over rice. **Yield:** 4 servings.

Turkey a la King

Prep/Total Time: 25 min.

Mary Gaylord • Balsam Lake, Wisconsin
These tasty bites look so cute served in pastry shells! They're a great way to use up leftover prepared turkey or chicken. You might want to make a double batch. No one can eat just one!

    1 medium onion, chopped
  3/4 cup sliced celery
  1/4 cup diced green pepper
  1/4 cup butter, cubed
  1/4 cup all-purpose flour
    1 teaspoon sugar
1-1/2 cups chicken broth
  1/4 cup half-and-half cream
    3 cups cubed cooked turkey *or* chicken
    1 can (4 ounces) sliced mushrooms, drained
    6 pastry shells *or* pieces of toast

In a large skillet, saute the onion, celery and green pepper in butter until tender. Stir in flour and sugar until a paste forms. Gradually stir in broth. Bring to a boil; boil 1 minute or until thickened. Reduce heat. Add cream, turkey and mushrooms; heat through. Serve either in pastry shells or over toast. **Yield:** 6 servings.

Skillet Chicken

Prep/Total Time: 30 min.

Wandalean Reagan • Baltimore, Maryland
I found this basic recipe on a package of chicken breasts. I made changes because my husband and I like more sauce than the original recipe provided.

    2 boneless skinless chicken breast halves
      (8 ounces *each*)
    1 tablespoon butter
  1/2 cup chopped onion
    1 can (14-1/2 ounces) diced tomatoes,
      undrained
    1 tablespoon Worcestershire sauce
  1/2 teaspoon ground mustard
  1/2 teaspoon salt
  1/8 to 1/4 teaspoon pepper
Hot cooked rice

In a large skillet, brown chicken in butter. Add onion; saute until tender. Stir in the tomatoes, Worcestershire sauce, mustard, salt and pepper. Bring to a boil over medium heat. Reduce heat; cover and simmer for 15 minutes or until chicken juices run clear. Serve over rice. **Yield:** 2 servings.

Cheddar Chicken Spirals

(Pictured below)
Prep/Total Time: 25 min.

Miriam Christophel • Battle Creek, Michigan
My granddaughters just love this chicken dish. I try to make it every time they come to visit. Lucky for me, it goes together quick as a wink.

1-1/2 cups uncooked spiral pasta
  1/2 cup mayonnaise
  1/3 cup milk
  1/2 teaspoon salt
  1/2 teaspoon dried basil
    2 cups frozen mixed vegetables, thawed
1-1/2 cups cubed cooked chicken
1-1/2 cups (6 ounces) shredded cheddar cheese,
      divided

Cook noodles according to package directions. Meanwhile, in a large bowl, combine the mayonnaise, milk, salt and basil. Stir in the vegetables, chicken and 1 cup cheese. Drain pasta; stir into vegetable mixture.

Transfer to a greased 1-1/2-qt. microwave-safe dish. Sprinkle with remaining cheese. Cover and microwave on high for 5-6 minutes or until heated through and the cheese is melted. Let stand for 5 minutes before serving. **Yield:** 4 servings.

Editor's Note: Reduced-fat or fat-free mayonnaise is not recommended for this recipe. This recipe was tested with an 850-watt microwave.

Cheddar Chicken Spirals

Pork Chops with Apples (p. 70)

Pork & Sausage

For supper in a snap, turn to quick cooking pork and sausage. Delicious items such as ham, pork chops and Italian sausage offer the savory tastes your family craves...without requiring much time in the kitchen.

Pork Slaw Skillet

Pork Slaw Skillet
(Pictured above)
Prep/Total Time: 20 min.

Jerry Harrison • St. Mary's, Georgia
Slices of pork tenderloin and a crispy homemade slaw combine in this delicious recipe. I've been serving it to family and friends for nearly 30 years, and it's still a hit.

> 2 pork tenderloins (about 3/4 pound *each*) cut into 1/4-inch slices
> 2 tablespoons vegetable oil
> Salt and pepper to taste
> SLAW:
> 1 tablespoon all-purpose flour
> 1/2 cup water
> 2 tablespoons cider vinegar
> 1 tablespoon sugar
> 1 tablespoon prepared mustard
> 2 teaspoons Worcestershire sauce
> 1 teaspoon salt
> 1/2 to 1 teaspoon celery seed
> Dash pepper
> 7 cups shredded cabbage
> 1-1/2 cups shredded carrots
> 1 medium onion, chopped
> 1 cup chopped green pepper, optional

In a large skillet, cook pork in oil over medium heat for 2-3 minutes on each side or until juices run clear. Season with salt and pepper. Remove and keep warm.

In a large bowl, combine the flour and water until smooth. Stir in the vinegar, sugar, mustard, Worcestershire sauce, salt, celery seed and pepper; pour into the skillet. Add vegetables. Cook and stir over medium heat until mixture comes to a boil. Cook and stir for 2 minutes or until thickened and vegetables are crisp-tender. Top with pork; cover and heat through. **Yield:** 4 servings.

Pork Chops With Apples
(Pictured on page 68)
Prep/Total Time: 30 min.

Marilou Robinson • Portland, Oregon
These moist, tender chops get delicious flavor from Dijon mustard, onions and apple slices. Or try replacing the apples with pineapple rings for an appealing variation. I like to serve the main course with mashed sweet potatoes and a simple salad.

> 4 bone-in pork loin chops (7 ounces *each* and 3/4-inch thick)
> 2 tablespoons vegetable oil
> 1/2 teaspoon salt
> 1/4 teaspoon pepper
> 2 medium onions, thinly sliced
> 1 large green apple, cut into thin wedges
> 1 large red apple, cut into thin wedges
> 2 tablespoons Dijon mustard
> 1 tablespoon brown sugar

In a large skillet, brown pork chops in oil on each side. Season with salt and pepper; remove and keep warm. In the same skillet, saute onions and apple wedges until crisp-tender. Combine mustard and brown sugar; brush over chops. Return to the skillet; cook for 4 minutes or until meat juices run clear. **Yield:** 4 servings.

Chops with Potato Gravy
Prep/Total Time: 25 min.

Marge Anderson • Fergus Falls, Minnesota
For a change-of-pace supper, I simmer pork chops in a white sauce made easy with a can of cream of potato soup. Served with noodles and a green salad it's a very filling meal for two.

> 2 bone-in pork loin chops (8 ounces *each*), cooked
> 1/2 teaspoon garlic salt
> 1/2 teaspoon poultry seasoning
> 1/8 to 1/4 teaspoon pepper
> 1 can (10-3/4 ounces) condensed cream of potato soup, undiluted

Place pork chops in a skillet; sprinkle with garlic salt, poultry seasoning and pepper. Carefully spread soup over the chops. Cover and cook over low heat for 20-25 minutes or until heated through. **Yield:** 2 servings.

Fancy Mac 'n' Cheese

(Pictured below)
Prep/Total Time: 30 min.

Janet Twigg • Campbellford, Ontario

For an update to an all-time classic, try this half-hour recipe. Cubed ham, broccoli and a golden topping make this dinnertime staple seem special without a lot of extra work.

 2 packages (7-1/4 ounces *each*) macaroni and white cheddar *or* cheddar cheese dinner mix
 2 cups fresh broccoli florets
 1/2 cup chopped onion
 2 garlic cloves, minced
 1/2 cup butter plus 1 tablespoon butter, *divided*
 1/2 cup milk
 2 cups cubed fully cooked ham
 1 tablespoon Dijon mustard
Salt and pepper to taste
 1 cup soft bread crumbs
 1/4 cup grated Parmesan cheese

Set cheese sauce packet from dinner mix aside. Bring 6 cups water to a boil. Add macaroni; cook for 4 minutes. Add the broccoli, onion and garlic. Cook 3-6 minutes longer or until macaroni is tender; drain.

In a large saucepan, melt 1/2 cup butter. Stir in cheese sauce mix and milk. Add ham, mustard, salt and pepper. Stir in macaroni mixture.

Transfer to a greased broiler-proof, 2-1/2-qt. baking dish. Melt remaining butter; toss with bread crumbs and Parmesan cheese. Sprinkle over top. Broil 4-6 in. from the heat for 4-5 minutes or until top is golden brown. **Yield:** 8 servings.

Fancy Mac 'n' Cheese

Tortellini Alfredo

Tortellini Alfredo

(Pictured above)
Prep/Total Time: 30 min.

Chris Snyder • Boulder, Colorado

I jazz up refrigerated tortellini with ham, mushrooms, peas and my homemade Alfredo sauce for a fast supper. When we're having company, I prepare the dinner shortly before guests arrive, put it in a casserole dish and keep it warm in the oven.

 2 packages (9 ounces *each*) refrigerated cheese tortellini
 1/2 cup chopped onion
 1/3 cup butter, cubed
 1-1/2 cups frozen peas, thawed
 1 cup thinly sliced fresh mushrooms
 1 cup cubed fully cooked ham
 1-3/4 cups heavy whipping cream
 1/4 teaspoon coarsely ground pepper
 3/4 cup grated Parmesan cheese
Shredded Parmesan cheese, optional

Cook tortellini according to package directions. Meanwhile, in a skillet, saute the onion in butter until tender. Add the peas, mushrooms and ham; cook until mushrooms are tender. Stir in cream and pepper; heat through. Stir in grated Parmesan cheese until melted.

Drain tortellini and place in a serving dish; add the sauce and toss to coat. Sprinkle with the shredded Parmesan cheese if desired. **Yield:** 4-6 servings.

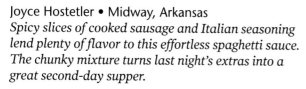

Italian Sausage Spaghetti

Barbecued Pork Chops

Prep/Total Time: 30 min.

David Bray • Hoover, Alabama
Try my homemade barbecue sauce the next time you're looking to season pork chops. We love this recipe because it's so easy to prepare in the microwave.

> 6 boneless pork loin chops (4 ounces *each* and 1/2 inch thick)
> 1 medium onion, chopped
> 1 cup ketchup
> 1/2 cup water
> 1/2 cup chopped celery
> 2 tablespoons lemon juice
> 1 tablespoon brown sugar
> 1 tablespoon Worcestershire sauce
> 1/2 teaspoon salt
> 1/2 teaspoon ground mustard
> 1 teaspoon cornstarch
> 1 tablespoon cold water

Place pork chops in an ungreased 11-in. x 7-in. x 2-in. microwave-safe dish.

In a large bowl, combine the next nine ingredients. Pour over the chops. Cover with plastic wrap; peel back one corner to vent. Microwave on high for 18-20 minutes or until juices run clear. Remove chops; set aside and keep warm.

In a small bowl, combine cornstarch and cold water until smooth. Stir into barbecue sauce. Microwave for 1 minute or until thickened. Serve sauce over chops. **Yield:** 6 servings.

Editor's Note: This recipe was tested with an 850-watt microwave.

Italian Sausage Spaghetti

(Pictured above)
Prep/Total Time: 30 min.

Joyce Hostetler • Midway, Arkansas
Spicy slices of cooked sausage and Italian seasoning lend plenty of flavor to this effortless spaghetti sauce. The chunky mixture turns last night's extras into a great second-day supper.

> 1 small onion, chopped
> 1 small green pepper, chopped
> 3 garlic cloves, minced
> 2 teaspoons olive oil
> 5 cooked Italian sausage links, cut into 1/4-inch slices
> 1 can (28 ounces) diced tomatoes, undrained
> 1 can (6 ounces) tomato paste
> 1/4 cup water
> 1 tablespoon Italian seasoning
> 1 teaspoon sugar
> 1/2 teaspoon salt
> 1/2 teaspoon pepper
> Hot cooked spaghetti

In a large saucepan, saute the onion, green pepper and garlic in oil tender. Stir in the sausage, tomatoes, tomato paste, water and seasonings. Bring to a boil. Reduce heat; cover and simmer for 15 minutes. Serve over spaghetti. **Yield:** 5 servings.

Sausage and Wild Rice

Prep/Total Time: 25 min.

Gaye Whittington • Leesville, South Carolina
Four ingredients are all you need for this family pleaser. Smoked sausage punches up the flavor.

> 1 package (6.2 ounces) long grain and wild rice mix
> 1 can (15 ounces) black beans, rinsed and drained
> 1 can (11 ounces) Mexicorn, drained
> 1/2 pound smoked sausage, cut into 1/2-inch slices

In a large skillet, prepare rice according to package directions. Add beans, corn and sausage. Cover and simmer for 10 minutes or until heated through. **Yield:** 4 servings.

Ham-Stuffed Squash Boats

Ham-Stuffed Squash Boats
(Pictured above)
Prep/Total Time: 30 min.

Fran Shaffer • Coatesville, Pennsylvania
Looking for a way to use up your bounty of summer squash or zucchini? Consider this idea, that fills the vegetables with ham, cheese and bread crumbs.

- 4 medium yellow summer squash *or* zucchini (about 6 inches)
- 1 small onion, finely chopped
- 2 tablespoons butter
- 1 cup cubed fully cooked ham
- 1/2 cup dry bread crumbs
- 1/2 cup shredded cheddar cheese
- 1/2 cup shredded Parmesan cheese, *divided*
- 1 egg, beaten
- 1 teaspoon paprika
- 1/4 teaspoon pepper

Cut squash in half lengthwise; scoop out pulp, leaving a 3/8-in. shell. Chop pulp and set aside.

In a large saucepan, cook shells in boiling water for 4-5 minutes. Drain and set aside. In another saucepan, saute onion in butter until tender; remove from the heat. Add ham, bread crumbs, cheddar cheese, 1/4 cup of Parmesan cheese, egg, paprika, pepper and squash pulp; mix well.

Spoon into shells. Place on a lightly greased baking sheet. Sprinkle with remaining Parmesan cheese. Bake at 425° for 12-15 minutes or until heated through. **Yield:** 4 servings.

Harvest Ham Skillet
(Pictured below)
Prep/Total Time: 30 min.

Jann Van Massenhoven • Hensall, Ontario
Speedy stovetop recipes are great ways to prepare ham. I rely on an eye-catching sauce that features diced apple, green onions and dried cranberries to give ordinary ham a special treatment.

- 1 tablespoon brown sugar
- 1-1/2 teaspoons cornstarch
- 2/3 cup apple juice
- 1-1/2 teaspoons Dijon mustard
- 1 teaspoon lemon juice
- 1 fully cooked ham slice (about 1-1/2 pounds and 1 inch thick), quartered
- 1 tablespoon butter
- 1 medium tart apple, peeled and diced
- 1/4 cup dried cranberries
- 2 green onions, chopped

In a small bowl, combine brown sugar and cornstarch. Stir in apple juice, mustard and lemon juice until smooth; set aside.

In a large skillet, brown the ham slice on both sides in butter. Remove and set aside. Add apple, cranberries and onions to the skillet; cook for 2-3 minutes or until apple is tender. Stir in the apple juice mixture. Bring to a boil; cook and stir for 2 minutes or until thickened. Return ham to the skillet; heat through. **Yield:** 4 servings.

Harvest Ham Skillet

Orange Pork Stir-Fry

Orange Pork Stir-Fry
(Pictured above)
Prep/Total Time: 30 min.

Wilma Jones • Mobile, Alabama
My family really loves this pretty stovetop supper. We have it often on weekends instead of going out for Chinese food.

  1 can (8 ounces) unsweetened pineapple chunks
  1 tablespoon brown sugar
  2 teaspoons cornstarch
1/4 cup chicken broth
  2 tablespoons lemon juice
  1 tablespoon reduced-sodium soy sauce
  1 teaspoon grated lemon peel
  1 pound pork tenderloin, cut into thin strips
  1 cup julienned sweet red *and/or* green pepper
  1 small onion, quartered and thinly sliced
  1 garlic clove, minced
1-1/2 teaspoons canola oil
  1 medium navel orange, peeled, sectioned and halved
  3 cups hot cooked rice

Drain pineapple, reserving juice; set juice and pineapple aside. In a bowl, combine brown sugar and cornstarch. Stir in the broth, lemon juice, soy sauce, lemon peel and reserved juice until blended; set aside.

In a nonstick skillet coated with nonstick cooking spray, stir-fry pork for 3-4 minutes or until meat is no longer pink; remove and keep warm.

In the same skillet, stir-fry pepper, onion and garlic in oil for 3-4 minutes or until crisp-tender. Stir the broth mixture; add to vegetables. Bring to a boil; cook and stir for 2 minutes. Return pork to the pan. Add orange pieces and pineapple; heat through. Serve over rice. **Yield:** 4 servings.

Creamy Ham Turnovers
(Pictured below)
Prep/Total Time: 30 min.

Earnestine Jackson • Beaumont, Texas
A tube of refrigerated dough helps make these tasty turnovers a real timesaver. The golden bundles look like you fussed, but they're very simple.

  4 ounces reduced-fat cream cheese, softened
  2 tablespoons fat-free milk
  1 teaspoon dill weed
  1 cup cubed fully cooked lean ham
  2 tablespoons diced onion
  1 celery rib, diced
  2 tablespoons diced pimientos
  1 tube (13.8 ounces) refrigerated pizza crust
  1 egg white, beaten

In a large mixing bowl, beat cream cheese, milk and dill until blended. Stir in the ham, onion, celery and pimientos. Roll out pizza dough into a 12-in. x 10-in. rectangle; cut in half lengthwise and widthwise. Place on a baking sheet coated with nonstick cooking spray.

Divide ham mixture evenly between the four rectangles. Fold opposite corners over ham mixture; pinch to seal. Brush with egg white. Bake at 400° for 20-25 minutes or until golden brown. **Yield:** 4 servings.

Creamy Ham Turnovers

Ham 'n' Cheese Bow Ties

Prep/Total Time: 30 min.

Stephanie Moon • Green Bay, Wisconsin
Everyone who tries this yummy casserole quickly lists it as a favorite from then on. Bow tie pasta makes it fun, and ham makes it hearty.

      1 garlic clove, minced
  1/4 cup butter, cubed
  1/4 cup all-purpose flour
  1/2 teaspoon salt
  1/8 teaspoon pepper
      2 cups milk
  1/2 teaspoon prepared mustard
2-1/2 cups (10 ounces) shredded Colby cheese
      2 cups uncooked bow tie pasta, cooked and drained
      6 to 8 ounces fully cooked ham, julienned
  1/4 cup grated Parmesan cheese

In a large saucepan, saute garlic in butter. Stir in flour, salt and pepper until blended. Gradually add milk. Bring to a boil; cook and stir for 2 minutes or until thickened and bubbly. Stir in the mustard and Colby cheese; cook and stir until cheese is melted. Add pasta and ham; stir until coated.

Transfer to a greased 2-qt. baking dish. Sprinkle with Parmesan cheese. Bake, uncovered, at 350° for 20-25 minutes or until heated through. **Yield:** 4-6 servings.

Herbed Pork Medallions

Prep/Total Time: 20 min.

Jodie Arkin • Waconia, Minnesota
It's hard to believe something this tasty comes together in less than a half hour. Brushed with honey, the herbed medallions easily turn last-minute suppers into memorable meals.

1-1/2 pounds pork tenderloin
      2 tablespoons butter, melted
  1/4 teaspoon garlic powder
  1/2 teaspoon salt
  1/2 teaspoon dried tarragon
  1/2 teaspoon dried thyme
  1/2 teaspoon paprika
  1/8 teaspoon pepper
  1/8 teaspoon cayenne pepper
      1 tablespoon honey

Cut pork into 1/2-in. slices and pound to flatten. Combine butter and garlic powder; brush over pork. Combine the seasonings; sprinkle over pork.

Place in two greased 15-in. x 10-in. x 1-in. baking

Sausage Squash Skillet

pans. Broil 4-6 in. from the heat for 5 minutes; turn and broil 3 minutes longer. Brush with honey; broil for 1 minute or until meat juices run clear. **Yield:** 6 servings.

Sausage Squash Skillet

(Pictured above)
Prep/Total Time: 15 min.

Marcia Albury • Severna Park, Maryland
I always thought yellow squash was bland until I prepared it this way. Combined with Italian sausage, it makes a delicious main dish in just minutes.

  1/2 pound bulk Italian sausage
  1/4 cup chopped onion
      1 medium yellow summer squash, halved and sliced
  1/4 cup chicken broth
Salt and pepper to taste
  1/3 cup seasoned salad croutons

In a large skillet over medium heat, cook sausage and onion until the meat is no longer pink; drain. Add the squash; cook for 3-4 minutes or until tender. Stir in the broth, salt and pepper. Cook 2 minutes longer or until heated through. Sprinkle with croutons. **Yield:** 2 servings.

Quick TIP
Bulk pork and Italian sausage are two ingredients that easily punch up the flavor of recipes. Use them to replace a quarter of the beef in your meat loaf, casserole or even breakfast bake and see for yourself.

Cranberry Pork Medallions

Cranberry Pork Medallions
(Pictured above)
Prep/Total Time: 20 min.

Maria Brennan • Waterbury, Connecticut
Juicy slices of pork tenderloin are matched with caramelized onions, rosemary and a delightful cranberry sauce that seems too good to be quick. No one suspects the dish is ready in less than half an hour.

- 1 pork tenderloin (about 1 pound), cut into 1/2-inch slices
- 3 tablespoons olive oil
- 1 medium onion, finely chopped
- 1 garlic clove, minced
- 3 tablespoons sugar
- 3/4 cup apple juice
- 1/2 cup cranberry juice
- 1/2 cup fresh *or* frozen cranberries, thawed
- 2 teaspoons Dijon mustard
- 1/2 teaspoon minced fresh rosemary *or* 1/8 teaspoon dried rosemary, crushed

Additional cranberries and fresh rosemary, optional

In a large nonstick skillet, cook pork in oil for 3-4 minutes on each side or until golden brown. Remove and set aside.

In the same skillet, saute onion, garlic and sugar until onion is caramelized and tender. Stir in the apple juice, cranberry juice, cranberries, mustard and rosemary. Bring to a boil. Reduce heat; simmer, uncovered, for 5-6 minutes or until sauce is reduced by half. Return pork to pan; heat through. Sprinkle with additional cranberries and rosemary if desired. **Yield:** 3 servings.

Gingered Pork Tenderloin

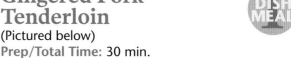
(Pictured below)
Prep/Total Time: 30 min.

Rebecca Evanoff • Holden, Massachusetts
Ginger, onions and garlic pack a flavorful punch paired with pork tenderloin. These tasty medallions smothered in golden caramelized onions are a simple and satisfying main dish.

- 2 large onions, thinly sliced
- 4 teaspoons olive oil
- 1/4 cup water
- 1 teaspoon ground ginger *or* 4 teaspoons minced fresh gingerroot
- 2 garlic cloves, minced
- 1/2 cup apple jelly
- 1 pork tenderloin (1 pound)
- 1/4 teaspoon salt

Hot cooked rice pilaf *or* rice

In a large skillet, saute onions in oil and water for 5-6 minutes. Stir in ginger and garlic. Cover and cook for 8-12 minutes or until onions are tender, stirring occasionally. Reduce heat; stir in apple jelly until melted.

Cut tenderloin into eight slices; flatten each to 1/2-in. thickness. Sprinkle with salt. In a large skillet coated with nonstick cooking spray, saute pork for 4 minutes; turn. Top with reserved onions; cover and cook for 5-7 minutes or until meat juices run clear. Serve with rice. **Yield:** 2-3 servings.

Gingered Pork Tenderloin

Hearty Ham Kabobs

Prep/Total Time: 30 min.

Gloria Houghton • Winter Park, Florida
A no-stress basting sauce gives these grilled skewers extra flair. Add a green salad or some garlic bread and dinner is served!

> 1 green pepper, cubed
> 1 medium onion, cut into wedges
> 2 cups cubed fully cooked ham (1-1/2-inch pieces)
> 12 cherry tomatoes
> 1 can (20 ounces) pineapple chunks, drained
> 1 cup bottled Italian salad dressing
> 1 teaspoon Worcestershire sauce
> Hot cooked rice

Blanch the green pepper and onion if desired. Thread alternately with the ham, tomatoes and pineapple onto four to six metal skewers.

Combine the salad dressing and Worcestershire sauce; baste over kabobs. Broil or grill, basting occasionally, until all ingredients are heated through, about 6-8 minutes. Serve over rice. **Yield:** 4-6 servings.

Pork Fried Rice

Prep/Total Time: 20 min.

Norma Reynolds • Overland Park, Kansas
My husband anxiously awaits the nights we have pork because he knows I'll use the leftovers in this recipe. Add some hot tea and a few fortune cookies to make the meal extra special.

> 1/2 cup diced carrots
> 1/2 cup diced celery
> 1/2 cup diced sweet red pepper
> 1/2 cup sliced green onions
> 2 tablespoons vegetable oil, *divided*
> 3 egg, lightly beaten
> 2 cups cubed cooked pork (about 1 pound)
> 2 cups cold cooked rice
> 4 to 5 teaspoons soy sauce
> Salt and pepper to taste

In a large skillet, saute the vegetables in 1 tablespoon of oil; remove and keep warm. Heat remaining oil over medium heat. Add eggs; cook and stir until set. Add the pork, rice, soy sauce, salt, pepper and vegetables; cook and stir until heated through. **Yield:** 5 servings.

Asparagus Ham Dinner

Asparagus Ham Dinner

(Pictured above)
Prep/Total Time: 25 min.

Rhonda Zavodny • David City, Nebraska
I've been making this one-dish dinner for my family for years now, and it's always well received. With asparagus, tomato, pasta and chunks of ham, it's a tempting blend of tastes and textures.

> 2 cups uncooked spiral pasta
> 3/4 pound fresh asparagus, cut into 1-inch pieces
> 1 medium sweet yellow pepper, julienned
> 1 tablespoon olive oil
> 3 cups diced fresh tomatoes (about 6 medium)
> 6 ounces reduced-sodium fully cooked ham, cubed
> 1/4 cup minced fresh parsley
> 1/2 teaspoon salt
> 1/2 teaspoon dried oregano
> 1/2 teaspoon dried basil
> 1/8 to 1/4 teaspoon cayenne pepper
> 1/4 cup shredded Parmesan cheese

Cook pasta according to package directions. Meanwhile, in a nonstick skillet, saute asparagus and yellow pepper in oil until tender. Add tomatoes and ham; heat through. Drain pasta; add to the vegetable mixture. Stir in seasonings. Sprinkle with Parmesan cheese. **Yield:** 6 servings.

Apricot-Glazed Shrimp (p. 80)

Fish & Seafood

From fish fillets and salmon steaks to crab cakes and shrimp stir-fries, seafood is a swift way to set a change-of-pace meal on the table. Swimming with flavor, these fast family favorites are sure to be hits in your home.

Maryland Crab Cakes

Maryland Crab Cakes
(Pictured above)
Prep/Total Time: 25 min.

Catherine Tocha • Silver Spring, Maryland
I've lived in Maryland for more than 50 years, so I know firsthand how much folks around here love crab cakes. I experimented with a number recipes before I came up with this quick and easy version. My family really likes it and I hope yours will, too.

      1 egg
  1/4 cup milk
      3 tablespoons mayonnaise
      1 tablespoon all-purpose flour
      1 tablespoon Worcestershire sauce
      1 teaspoon prepared mustard
      1 teaspoon salt
  1/4 teaspoon pepper
      1 pound cooked crabmeat *or* 3 cans
          (6 ounces *each*) crabmeat, drained,
          flaked and cartilage removed
  1/2 cup dry bread crumbs
      2 tablespoons butter

In a large bowl, whisk together the first eight ingredients. Fold in crab.

Place the bread crumbs in a shallow dish. Drop 1/3 cup crab mixture into crumbs; shape into a 3/4-in. thick patty. Carefully turn to coat. Repeat with remaining crab mixture.

In a large skillet, cook patties in butter for 3 minutes on each side or until golden brown. **Yield:** 6 patties.

Apricot-Glazed Shrimp

(Pictured on page 78)
Prep/Total Time: 20 min.

Aletha Graves • Bellingham, Washington
My husband has always been a beef eater, but after 53 years, I've finally gotten him to eat seafood. Sometimes I substitute cubed pork for the shrimp in this dish, but that's excellent, too!

      2 teaspoons cornstarch
  1/2 cup chicken broth
      3 tablespoons apricot preserves
      1 tablespoon reduced-sodium soy sauce
      1 teaspoon sesame seeds, toasted
      1 medium green pepper, julienned
      1 medium sweet red pepper, julienned
  1/4 cup sliced green onions
      1 garlic clove, minced
      2 teaspoons canola oil
  1/2 pound uncooked medium shrimp, peeled
          and deveined
  1/2 cup sliced water chestnuts, drained
  1-1/2 cups hot cooked rice

In a large bowl, combine the cornstarch, broth, preserves, soy sauce and sesame seeds until blended; set aside.

In a large nonstick skillet or wok, stir-fry the peppers, onions and garlic in oil for 5 minutes or until crisp-tender. Add shrimp and water chestnuts; stir-fry until shrimp turn pink. Stir broth mixture; add to the pan. Bring to a boil; cook and stir for 1-2 minutes or until thickened. Serve over rice. **Yield:** 2 servings.

Baked Parmesan Perch
Prep/Total Time: 20 min.

Carol Gaus • Itasca, Illinois
Bread crumbs, Parmesan cheese and basil make a crispy coating for fish fillets. We use it with perch, but try it with whatever fillets you like best.

      2 tablespoons dry bread crumbs
      1 tablespoon grated Parmesan cheese
      1 tablespoon paprika
      1 teaspoon dried basil
      1 pound perch *or* fish fillets of your choice
      1 tablespoon butter, melted

In a shallow bowl, combine the bread crumbs, Parmesan cheese, paprika and basil. Brush fish fillets with butter, then dip into the crumb mixture. Place in a greased baking pan. Bake, uncovered, at 500° for 10 minutes or until fish flakes easily with a fork. **Yield:** 4 servings.

Pecan-Crusted Salmon

(Pictured below)
Prep/Total Time: 25 min.

Cheryl Bykowski • Punta Gorda, Florida
My husband was thrilled the first time I served salmon with this nutty coating and refreshing cucumber sauce. I was happy that I could make something this good in no time flat.

- 2 salmon fillets (6 ounces *each*)
- 2 tablespoons mayonnaise
- 1/2 cup finely chopped pecans
- 1/3 cup seasoned bread crumbs
- 2 tablespoons grated Parmesan cheese
- 1 tablespoon minced fresh parsley
- 1 tablespoon butter, melted

CUCUMBER SAUCE:
- 1/2 cup chopped seeded peeled cucumber
- 1/2 cup vanilla yogurt
- 1/2 teaspoon snipped fresh dill *or*
  - 1/8 teaspoon dill weed
- 1/8 teaspoon garlic powder

Place salmon skin side down in a greased 11-in. x 7-in. x 2-in. baking dish. Spread 1 tablespoon mayonnaise over each fillet.

In a small bowl, combine the pecans, bread crumbs, Parmesan cheese, parsley and butter; spoon over salmon. Bake at 425° for 10-15 minutes or until fish flakes easily with a fork.

Meanwhile, in a small bowl, combine the cucumber sauce ingredients. Serve with the salmon. **Yield:** 2 servings.

Crunchy-Coated Walleye

Crunchy-Coated Walleye

(Pictured above)
Prep/Total Time: 20 min.

Sondra Ostheimer • Boscobel, Wisconsin
The secret to this speedy coating is combining mashed potato flakes with a few seasonings. Best of all, you can set it on the table in less than a half hour.

- 1/3 cup all-purpose flour
- 1 teaspoon paprika
- 1/2 teaspoon salt
- 1/4 teaspoon pepper
- 1/4 teaspoon onion powder
- 1/4 teaspoon garlic powder
- 2 eggs
- 2-1/4 pounds walleye, perch *or* pike fillets
- 1-1/2 cups mashed potato flakes
- 1/3 cup vegetable oil

Tartar sauce and lemon wedges, optional

In a shallow bowl, combine flour, paprika, salt, pepper, onion powder and garlic powder. In another bowl, beat the eggs. Dip both sides of fillets in flour mixture and eggs, then coat with potato flakes.

In a large skillet, fry fillets in oil for 5 minutes on each side or until fish flakes easily with a fork. Serve with tartar sauce and lemon if desired. **Yield:** 4 servings.

Pecan-Crusted Salmon

Flavorful Catfish Fillets

Scallops and Asparagus Stir-Fry

(Pictured below)
Prep/Total Time: 15 min.

Lisa Lancaster • Tracy, California
Savory scallops, crisp-tender asparagus and juicy cherry tomatoes blend together beautifully in this fresh-tasting stir-fry. Sesame oil and soy sauce accent the colorful combo.

    3/4 pound fresh asparagus, trimmed and cut
         into 2-inch pieces
      1 tablespoon cornstarch
    3/4 cup chicken broth
      1 teaspoon reduced-sodium soy sauce
    3/4 pound sea scallops, halved
      1 cup sliced fresh mushrooms
      1 garlic clove, minced
      2 teaspoons canola oil
      1 cup halved cherry tomatoes
      2 green onions, sliced
      1 teaspoon sesame oil
    1/8 teaspoon pepper
      2 cups hot cooked rice

Place asparagus in a saucepan and cover with water; bring to a boil. Cook, uncovered, for 3-5 minutes or until crisp-tender; drain and set aside. In a small bowl, combine the cornstarch, broth and soy sauce until smooth; set aside.

In a large nonstick skillet or wok, stir-fry scallops, mushrooms and garlic in canola oil until scallops are opaque and mushrooms are tender. Stir cornstarch mixture; add to skillet. Bring to a boil; cook and stir until sauce is thickened.

Add the asparagus, tomatoes, onions, sesame oil and pepper; heat through. Serve over rice. **Yield:** 4 servings.

Flavorful Catfish Fillets

(Pictured above)
Prep/Total Time: 15 min.

Ellen Munnik • Chesterfield, Michigan
This is the best catfish ever! It's fast to prepare, and the cayenne adds a little zip. The golden cornmeal and herb coating keeps the fillets moist and offers plenty of appeal without the fat that comes with frying.

    1/4 cup buttermilk
      2 teaspoons Dijon mustard
    1/2 cup cornmeal
      1 teaspoon *each* salt, onion powder, garlic
         powder and paprika
    1/2 teaspoon dried thyme
    1/2 teaspoon pepper
    1/4 to 1/2 teaspoon cayenne pepper
      1 pound catfish fillets
Lemon wedges, optional

In a shallow bowl, whisk buttermilk and mustard until smooth. In another bowl, combine the cornmeal and seasonings. Dip fillets into buttermilk mixture, then into cornmeal mixture.

Place 1 in. apart on a wire rack coated with nonstick cooking spray. Place rack on a baking sheet. Broil 4 in. from the heat for 3-4 minutes on each side or until fish flakes easily with a fork. Serve with lemon if desired. **Yield:** 4 servings.

Scallops and Asparagus Stir-Fry

Four-Seafood Fettuccine

Prep/Total Time: 30 min.

Jeri Dobrowski • Beach, North Dakota
Here's an easy entree that tastes like you spent hours in the kitchen. Loaded with crabmeat, clams, lobster and shrimp, it's one dish that'll please everyone at the dinner table.

```
12  ounces fettuccine
 2  garlic cloves, minced
 3  tablespoons butter
 3  tablespoons all-purpose flour
 1  cup milk
 1  can (12 ounces) evaporated milk
 1  cup crabmeat, drained, flaked and
    cartilage removed
 1  cup cooked or canned lobster, drained and
    chopped
 1  can (6-1/2 ounces) chopped clams, drained
 1  can (4-1/2 ounces) tiny shrimp, drained
1/2 cup shredded Parmesan cheese
 1  tablespoon minced fresh parsley
1/4 teaspoon pepper
```

Cook fettuccine according to package directions.
Meanwhile, in a large saucepan, saute garlic in butter. Stir in flour until blended. Gradually add milk and evaporated milk. Bring to a boil; cook and stir for 2 minutes or thickened. Add the crab, lobster, clams, shrimp, Parmesan cheese, parsley and pepper; heat through. Drain fettuccine; top with seafood mixture. **Yield:** 6 servings.

Glazed Orange Roughy

Prep/Total Time: 25 min.

Jo Baker • Litchfield, Illinois
Dijon mustard and apricot fruit spread create a golden glaze for fish fillets in this fast entree. It's hard to believe it only calls for four ingredients.

```
 4  fresh or frozen orange roughy fillets
    (4 ounces each)
1/4 cup apricot spreadable fruit or orange
    marmalade
 2  teaspoons butter, melted
 2  teaspoons Dijon mustard
```

Place fillets on an ungreased shallow baking pan. Broil 4-6 in. from the heat for 5-6 minutes. Combine spreadable fruit, butter and mustard; spoon over fillets. Broil 3-4 minutes longer or until fish flakes easily with a fork (do not turn). **Yield:** 4 servings.

Trout Baked in Cream

Trout Baked in Cream
(Pictured above)
Prep/Total Time: 20 min.

Ann Nace • Perkasie, Pennsylvania
Here's a quick and delicious way to serve trout. It's definitely one of our family's favorites. I hope your gang likes it, too.

```
 6  trout fillets (about 3-1/2 ounces each)
 2  tablespoons lemon juice
 1  teaspoon dill weed
1/2 teaspoon salt
1/8 teaspoon pepper
 1  cup heavy whipping cream
 2  tablespoons seasoned bread crumbs
```

Place trout in a greased 13-in. x 9-in. x 2-in. baking dish. Sprinkle with lemon juice, dill, salt and pepper. Pour cream over all. Sprinkle with bread crumbs. Bake, uncovered, at 350° for 11-15 minutes or until the fish flakes easily with a fork. **Yield:** 4-6 servings.

Quick TIP Shrimp is lifesaver for busy family cooks. Not only does it cook up in minutes, but its versatility makes it a breeze to please everyone's palate. Add cooked shrimp to your stir-fries on casseroles for fast flavor.

Tuna Crunch Casserole

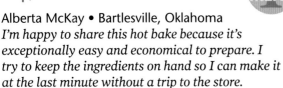

Prep/Total Time: 30 min.

Alberta McKay • Bartlesville, Oklahoma
*I'm happy to share this hot bake because it's
exceptionally easy and economical to prepare. I
try to keep the ingredients on hand so I can make it
at the last minute without a trip to the store.*

  1/4 cup sliced almonds
    1 small onion, chopped
    1 celery rib, chopped
    2 tablespoons butter
    2 cups shredded cabbage
    1 can (6-1/8 ounces) tuna, drained
    1 can (10-3/4 ounces) condensed cream of
        mushroom soup, undiluted
    1 can (3 ounces) chow mein noodles, *divided*

In a large skillet, saute the almonds, onion and celery in butter. Meanwhile, in a large bowl, combine the cabbage, tuna, soup and half of the chow mein noodles. Stir in almond mixture.

Spoon into an ungreased 11-in. x 7-in. x 2-in. baking dish. Sprinkle remaining noodles on top. Bake at 350° for 20 minutes or until bubbly. **Yield:** 6 servings.

Baked Shrimp And Asparagus

(Pictured below)
Prep/Total Time: 30 min.

Jane Rhodes • Silverdale, Washington
*I invented this casserole when I needed to serve 30
co-workers at a holiday party. I knew it was a hit when
people asked for the recipe. I've since pared it down so
I can make it more often. It tastes special, yet it's fast to
fix on busy weeknights.*

Baked Shrimp and Asparagus

    1 package (12 ounces) frozen cut asparagus
    1 pound uncooked medium shrimp, peeled
        and deveined
    1 can (10-3/4 ounces) condensed cream of
        shrimp soup, undiluted
    1 tablespoon butter, melted
    1 teaspoon soy sauce
  1/2 cup salad croutons, optional
Hot cooked rice

In a large bowl, combine the first five ingredients. Spoon into a greased 8-in. square baking dish.

Bake, uncovered, at 425° for 20 minutes or until shrimp turn pink. Top with croutons if desired; bake 5 minutes longer. Serve over rice. **Yield:** 4-6 servings.

Favorite Halibut Casserole

Prep/Total Time: 30 min.

Gayle Brown • Millville, Utah
*I've been using this recipe since my college days. You
can substitute any whitefish for the halibut. With
cheese and a bubbling sauce, it's pure comfort food.*

    5 tablespoons butter, *divided*
  1/4 cup all-purpose flour
  1/2 teaspoon salt
  1/8 to 1/4 teaspoon white pepper
1-1/2 cups milk
    1 small green pepper, chopped
    1 small onion, chopped
    2 cups cubed cooked halibut (about 1
        pound)
    3 hard-cooked eggs, chopped
    1 jar (2 ounces) diced pimientos, drained
  1/3 cup shredded cheddar cheese

In a large saucepan, melt 4 tablespoons butter. Stir in flour, salt and pepper until smooth. Gradually add milk. Bring to a boil; cook and stir for 2 minutes or until thickened. Remove from heat; cover and set aside.

In a small skillet, saute green pepper and onion in remaining butter until tender. Stir into white sauce. Add the halibut, eggs and pimientos.

Transfer to a greased 1-1/2-qt. baking dish. Sprinkle with cheese. Bake, uncovered, at 375° for 15-20 minutes or until bubbly. **Yield:** 4 servings.

Batter-Fried Fish

(Pictured below)
Prep/Total Time: 15 min.

Nancy Johnson • Connersville, Indiana
Whether I'm fixing cod fillets or my husband's catch of the day, this batter makes the fish fry up golden and crispy. Club soda gives it a different twist...and the sweet and zippy sauce complements the fish nicely. If you don't have time to make the sauce, simply open a jar of tartar sauce.

>   1/2 pound fresh *or* frozen cod fillets
>   2 tablespoons all-purpose flour
>   2 to 3 tablespoons cornstarch
>   1/4 teaspoon *each* garlic powder, onion powder, salt, cayenne pepper and paprika
>   1/8 teaspoon dried oregano
>   1/8 teaspoon dried thyme
>   1/3 cup club soda
> Oil for frying
>   1/4 cup orange marmalade
>   1 to 2 tablespoons prepared horseradish

Rinse fillets in cold water; pat dry. Coat with flour. In a shallow bowl, combine the cornstarch, seasonings and soda. In a heavy skillet, heat 1 in. of oil. Dip floured fillets into batter; fry over medium heat for 2-3 minutes on each side or until the fish flakes easily with a fork. Combine marmalade and horseradish; spoon over fish. **Yield:** 2 servings.

Italian-Style Walleye

Italian-Style Walleye

(Pictured above)
Prep/Total Time: 25 min.

Cathy Lueschen • Columbus, Nebraska
Herbs and melted cheese dress up fillets in my speedy recipe. When I want a quick fish dinner, it's the dish I turn to most.

>   4 to 6 walleye fillets (about 1-1/2 pounds)
>   1 can (15 ounces) tomato sauce
>   2 tablespoons chopped fresh parsley
>   1 teaspoon Italian seasoning
>   1/2 teaspoon dried basil
>   1/4 teaspoons salt
>   1/8 teaspoon pepper
>   1 cup (4 ounces) shredded part-skim mozzarella cheese

Place walleye in a greased shallow 3-qt. or 13-in. x 9-in. x 2-in. baking dish. In a small bowl, combine tomato sauce, parsley, Italian seasoning, basil, salt and pepper; pour over the fish.

Bake, uncovered, at 350° for 15 minutes. Sprinkle with mozzarella cheese. Bake 5-10 minutes longer or until fish flakes easily with a fork. **Yield:** 4-6 servings.

Batter-Fried Fish

Quick TIP Keep frozen fish fillets on hand for fast meals. Whether they are baked, broiled or pan-fried, the boneless pieces of fish are table-ready in mere moments. You can even make them into a warm sandwich if you'd like.

Spicy Shrimp Fettuccine

(Pictured below)
Prep/Total Time: 30 min.

Judy Farrar • Richmond, Virginia
Here's a way to make a tasty impression on family and friends. Nicely spiced shrimp, tomatoes and spinach top off saucy fettuccine in the streamlined supper. Try it alongside freshly sliced bread and salad greens.

      8 ounces uncooked fettuccine
      1 medium onion, chopped
      1 garlic clove, minced
      1 tablespoon olive oil
      4 plum tomatoes, chopped
      1 cup chicken broth
      2 cups coarsely chopped fresh spinach
    3/4 pound cooked medium shrimp, peeled and
         deveined
      2 tablespoons minced fresh parsley
      1 tablespoon balsamic vinegar
      1 tablespoon butter
    1/2 teaspoon salt
    1/4 teaspoon pepper
    1/8 teaspoon cayenne pepper
      2 ounces feta cheese, crumbled

Cook fettuccine according to package directions.

Meanwhile, in a large nonstick skillet, saute onion and garlic in oil until tender. Add tomatoes and broth. Bring to a boil. Reduce heat; simmer, uncovered, for 3 minutes. Add the spinach, shrimp, parsley and vinegar. Simmer, uncovered, for 2 minutes or until shrimp is heated through. Stir in the butter, salt, pepper and cayenne. Drain fettuccine; top with shrimp mixture and feta cheese. **Yield:** 4 servings.

Spicy Shrimp Fettuccine

Mountain Trout With Butter Sauce

Prep/Total Time: 20 min.

Pauletta Boese • Macon, Mississippi
Recently, we hosted a group of young people from Canada. Since we wanted to give them a true taste of the South, I served this seafood specialty. They raved about it, and I didn't have to spend hours preparing it.

      3 pounds mountain trout fillets, cut into
         4-ounce portions
    Salt and pepper to taste
      1 cup all-purpose flour
    1/2 cup olive oil
    1/2 cup butter
    Juice of 2 lemons
    1/2 cup chicken *or* brown gravy, optional

Season trout with salt and pepper; dredge with flour. Heat oil in a skillet. Saute trout quickly in hot oil, browning evenly on both sides.

Remove trout to a shallow baking pan. Bake at 350° for 5-10 minutes or until fish flakes easily with a fork; keep warm.

Meanwhile, in a saucepan, heat butter until butter begins to brown. Carefully add lemon juice (hot butter will bubble when juice is added). Stir in gravy if desired. Spoon sauce over fish or serve on the side. **Yield:** 6 servings.

Quick Crab Mornay

Prep/Total Time: 30 min.

Geneva Schmidtka • Canandaigua, New York
A rich, cheesy sauce showcases canned crabmeat in this dish. The creamy mixture can be served with toast points or over rice or potatoes for a distinctive dinner.

      1 can (10-3/4 ounces) condensed cream of
         chicken soup, undiluted
    1/3 cup white wine *or* chicken broth
      1 egg, lightly beaten
      1 can (6 ounces) crabmeat, drained, flaked
         and cartilage removed
    1/2 cup shredded cheddar cheese

In a small saucepan, combine soup and wine or broth. Cook and stir over medium heat until blended and heated through. Stir 1/2 cup of soup mixture into the egg; return all to the pan.

Place the crab in a greased shallow 1-qt. baking dish; top with soup mixture. Sprinkle with cheese. Bake, uncovered, at 350° for 20 minutes or until the top is lightly browned and cheese is melted. **Yield:** 4-6 servings.

Firecracker Salmon Steaks

(Pictured below)
Prep/Total Time: 20 min.

Phyllis Schmalz • Kansas City, Kansas
Red pepper flakes and cayenne pepper provide fiery flavor that gives these salmon steaks their name. Basting the fish with the zippy sauce while grilling creates a pretty glaze.

- 1/4 cup balsamic vinegar
- 1/4 cup chili sauce
- 1/4 cup packed brown sugar
- 3 garlic cloves, minced
- 2 teaspoons minced fresh parsley
- 1 teaspoon minced fresh gingerroot
- 1/4 to 1/2 teaspoon cayenne pepper
- 1/4 to 1/2 teaspoon crushed red pepper flakes, optional
- 4 salmon steaks (6 ounces *each*)

Coat grill rack with nonstick cooking spray before starting the grill. In a small bowl, combine the vinegar, chili sauce, sugar, garlic, parsley and seasonings. Grill salmon, covered, over medium heat for 4-5 minutes on each side or until fish flakes easily with a fork, brushing occasionally with sauce. **Yield:** 4 servings.

Editor's Note: To broil the salmon, place on a broiler pan. Broil 4-6 in. from the heat for 4-5 minutes on each side or until fish flakes easily with a fork, brushing occasionally with sauce.

Firecracker Salmon Steaks

Seafood Fettuccine

Seafood Fettuccine

(Pictured above)
Prep/Total Time: 15 min.

Kim Jorgensen • Coulee City, Washington
Loaded with shrimp and mushrooms, this no-stress dinner solution is one you'll reach for time and again. It's a great meal-in-one that always satisfies. It even impresses company.

- 3/4 pound uncooked medium shrimp, peeled and deveined
- 1 can (4 ounces) mushroom stems and pieces, drained
- 1/2 teaspoon garlic powder
- 1/8 teaspoon salt
- 1/8 teaspoon pepper
- 1/4 cup butter, cubed
- 1 package (8 ounces) fettuccine, cooked and drained
- 1/2 cup grated Parmesan cheese
- 1/2 cup milk
- 1/2 cup sour cream

Minced fresh parsley, optional

In a large saucepan, saute shrimp, mushrooms, garlic powder, salt and pepper in butter for 3-5 minutes. Stir in fettuccine, Parmesan cheese, milk and sour cream. Cook over medium heat for 3-5 minutes or until heated through (do not boil). Sprinkle with parsley if desired. **Yield:** 4 servings.

Editor's Note: Scallops or crab may be substituted for half of the shrimp.

Lemon Chicken
Quick Fruit Salad
Herb Bread (p. 95)

30-Minute Meals

**Have a swarming schedule? There's still time
to set a complete, three-item meal on the table.
Let the six menus featured in this chapter show you
how. Each dinner can prepared in just half an hour.**

ENJOY A SEAFOOD SUPPER IN A SNAP

Crab-Topped Fish Fillets
Prep/Total Time: 30 min.

Mary Tuthill • Ft. Myers Beach, Florida
Elegant but truly no bother, this recipe is perfect for company but easy enough for weekdays. Toasting the almonds gives them a little more crunch, which is a delightful way to top the fish fillets.

    4 sole, orange roughy *or* cod fillet (6 ounces each)
    1 can (6 ounces) crabmeat, drained, flaked and cartilage removed *or* 1 cup imitation crabmeat, chopped
  1/2 cup grated Parmesan cheese
  1/2 cup mayonnaise
    1 teaspoon lemon juice
Paprika, optional
  1/3 cup slivered almonds, toasted

Place fillets in a greased 13-in. x 9-in. x 2-in. baking dish. Bake, uncovered, at 350° for 18-22 minutes or until fish flakes easily with a fork. Meanwhile, in a bowl, combine the crab, Parmesan cheese, mayonnaise and lemon juice.

Drain cooking juices from baking dish; spoon crab mixture over fillets. Broil 5 in. from the heat for 5 minutes or until topping is lightly browned. Sprinkle with paprika if desired and almonds. **Yield:** 4 servings.

Three-Cheese Potato Bake
Prep/Total Time: 30 min.

Lois Buffalow • Grandview, Missouri
For a comforting potato dish that's ready in no time, consider creamy Three-Cheese Potato Bake. It's hard to get this sort of a satisfying side with a fast recipe, so this casserole is a keeper.

2-2/3 cups chicken broth
  2/3 cup milk
  1/4 cup butter, cubed
  1/4 teaspoon pepper
2-2/3 cups mashed potato flakes
  1/3 cup shredded Monterey Jack cheese
  1/3 cup shredded cheddar cheese
  1/3 cup cubed process cheese (Velveeta)
    2 tablespoons snipped chives
  1/4 cup sour cream, optional

In a large saucepan, combine the broth, milk, butter and pepper; bring to a boil. Remove from the heat; stir in potato flakes. Let stand for 30 seconds; fluff with a fork.

Transfer to a greased 1-qt. baking dish. Top with cheeses. Bake, uncovered, at 350° for 20 minutes or until cheese is melted. Sprinkle with chives. Serve with sour cream if desired. **Yield:** 4 servings.

Green Beans with Radishes
Prep/Total Time: 20 min.

Marlene Muckenhirn • Delano, Minnesota
Here's a side dish with a full-flavored twist. The fresh beans are so pretty mixed with crisp radish slices. It's as good with chicken as it is with fish.

  1 pound fresh green beans, trimmed
  2 tablespoons thinly sliced green onion
  2 tablespoons butter
  1 teaspoon lemon juice
  1 teaspoon soy sauce
1/4 cup sliced radishes

Place beans in a large saucepan and cover with water; bring to a boil. Cook, uncovered, for 8-10 minutes or until crisp-tender; drain.

In a large skillet, saute onion in butter just until tender. Stir in the beans, lemon juice and soy sauce; cook and stir until heated through. Just before serving, sprinkle with radishes. **Yield:** 4 servings.

REFRESHING SALAD-SANDWICH COMBO LIVENS UP SUMMER DINING

For Nanci Keatley of Salem, Oregon, a delightful meal doesn't mean spending a lot of time in the kitchen. Here, she shares her secret to fuss-free cooking with a warm and easy sandwich, crispy green salad and cute, little desserts.

"While the ingredients are ideal for warm-weather suppers, this is a wonderful meal any time of the year," Nanci says. "It makes a great dinner as well as a hearty lunch. In fact, I even served the menu at a ladies' luncheon that I once hosted."

Loaded with berries, the individual trifles are a fun way to cap off any meal, but you can layer all of the ingredients in one serving bowl as well. "The 15-minute trifle is a mainstay on my potluck list," explains Nanci. "Feel free to try it with peaches or even necatrines if you have them on hand instead of the berries."

Orange Romaine Salad
Prep/Total Time: 15 min.

- 8 cups torn romaine
- 1 can (11 ounces) mandarin oranges, drained *or* 2 medium oranges, peeled and sliced
- 1 cup thinly sliced red onion
- 1/4 cup red wine vinegar
- 3 tablespoons olive oil
- 1 tablespoon minced fresh parsley
- 1 garlic clove, minced

Salt and pepper to taste

In a large bowl, combine romaine, oranges and onion. Combine remaining ingredients; pour over salad and toss to coat. Serve immediately. **Yield:** 4-6 servings.

Lemon Berry Trifle
Prep/Total Time: 15 min.

- 5 cups cubed angel food cake
- 1 carton (8 ounces) lemon yogurt
- 1 cup whipping topping, *divided*
- 3 cups mixed fresh berries

Lemon peel, optional

Place cake cubes in a 2-qt. serving bowl or individual dishes. Combine yogurt and 3/4 cup whipped topping; spoon over cake. Top with berries. Top with remaining whipped topping and lemon peel if desired. **Yield:** 4-6 servings.

Italian Subs
Prep/Total Time: 15 min.

- 1 loaf (8 ounces) French bread
- 6 slices part-skim mozzarella cheese, *divided*
- 12 thin slices fully cooked ham *or* turkey
- 1 medium tomato, thinly sliced
- 1 tablespoon olive oil
- 2 teaspoons red wine vinegar
- 2-1/2 teaspoons dried basil
- 1/8 teaspoon pepper
- 1/8 teaspoon dried rosemary, crushed

Cut bread in half horizontally; set top aside. Place three slices of cheese on bottom half; layer with ham and tomato.

In a small bowl, combine oil, vinegar, basil, pepper and rosemary; drizzle over tomato. Top with remaining cheese.

Broil 4 in. from the heat for 2-3 minutes or until cheese is melted. Replace bread top. Cut into four pieces; serve immediately. **Yield:** 4 servings.

STROGANOFF STARS IN HALF-HOUR MENU

Microwave Stroganoff
Prep/Total Time: 30 min.

DISH MEAL

Karen Kurtz • Muskegon, Michigan
My microwave makes mealtime a breeze, particularly with mouth-watering recipes like this. Onion soup mix makes the meat so savory. Served over noodles, the creamy stroganoff is comfort food at its best.

>   2 tablespoons butter
> 1-1/2 pounds boneless beef sirloin steak, cut into
>   thin strips
>   1/4 cup all-purpose flour
>   1 envelope onion soup mix
> 2-1/4 cups hot water
>   1 can (4 ounces) mushroom stems and
>   pieces, drained
>   1/2 cup sour cream
> Hot cooked noodles

Melt butter in a 2-qt. microwave-safe dish; arrange meat evenly in dish. Microwave, uncovered, on high for 6 minutes, stirring once. Remove meat with a slotted spoon and keep warm.

Stir flour and soup mix into drippings until blended. Gradually add water, stirring until smooth. Add mushrooms and beef.

Cover and microwave on high for 18 minutes or until the meat is tender and the sauce is thickened, stirring several times and rotating a half turn once. Stir in the sour cream. Serve with noodles. **Yield:** 6-8 servings.

Editor's Note: This recipe was tested with an 850-watt microwave.

Wilted Lettuce Salad
Prep/Total Time: 15 min.

Cheryl Newendorp • Pella, Iowa
A few moments are all you need for a warm dressing that's just perfect over leaf lettuce. After one bite, you'll want to add this recipe to holiday menus as well as weeknight suppers.

>   6 cups torn leaf lettuce
>   3 tablespoons finely chopped onion
>   3 bacon strips, diced
>   2 tablespoons red wine vinegar
> 2-1/4 teaspoons sugar
> 1-1/2 teaspoons water
> Salt and pepper to taste
>   1 hard-cooked egg, sliced

In a large salad bowl, combine the lettuce and onion; set aside.

Place the bacon in a microwave-safe dish; cover with a microwave-safe paper towel. Cook on high for 5 minutes or until crisp, stirring every 30 seconds. Using a slotted spoon, remove bacon to paper towels.

In a small microwave-safe dish, combine 1-1/2 teaspoons bacon drippings, vinegar, sugar and water.

Microwave, uncovered, on high for 1 minute. Pour over lettuce; sprinkle with salt and pepper. Add bacon and egg; toss to coat. **Yield:** 6 servings.

Editor's Note: This recipe was tested with an 850-watt microwave.

Apricot Pecan Sauce
Prep/Total Time: 10 min.

Eleanor Martens • Rosenort, Manitoba
Who would have thought that a heavenly sauce like this could come together so quickly? Used as a topping for ice cream, it's a perfectly easy way to cap off a lovely, work-night dinner.

>   1/2 cup apricot spreadable fruit
>   1/2 cup heavy whipping cream
>   2 tablespoons butter
>   1/2 cup chopped pecans
>   1/2 teaspoon vanilla extract
>   1/4 to 1 teaspoon rum extract, optional
> Vanilla ice cream

In a large saucepan, combine the spreadable fruit, cream and butter. Bring to a boil. Reduce heat; simmer, uncovered, for 3-5 minutes or until blended. Stir in pecans, vanilla and rum extract if desired. Remove from the heat. Serve over ice cream. **Yield:** 1 cup.

BUSY MOM CREATES STOVETOP SENSATION

In Bloomsburg, Pennsylvania, Tracy Golder values meals she can set on the table in a jiffy. "Sometimes it seems as though there isn't enough time in the day," she notes, "so I look for quick menus.

"Chili Mac Skillet comes together in moments and thanks to convenience items, I can mix up the corn bread and kid-friendly dessert in no time," she adds.

Chili Mac Skillet
Prep/Total Time: 15 min.

1-1/4 cups uncooked elbow macaroni
   1 pound ground beef
   1 medium onion, chopped
   1 medium green pepper, chopped
   2 garlic cloves, minced
   2 cans (14-1/2 ounces *each*) diced tomatoes, undrained
   1 can (16 ounces) kidney beans, rinsed and drained
   1 package (10 ounces) frozen corn, thawed
   2 tablespoons chili powder
 1/2 to 1 teaspoon salt
 1/2 teaspoon ground cumin
 1/2 cup shredded pepper Jack cheese

Cook the macaroni according to the package directions.

Meanwhile, in a large skillet, cook the beef, onion, green pepper and garlic over medium heat until meat is no longer pink and vegetables are tender; drain. Stir in the tomatoes, beans, corn, chili powder, salt and cumin. Bring to a boil. Reduce heat; cover and simmer for 15 minutes or until heated through.

Drain the macaroni and add to skillet; stir to coat. Sprinkle with cheese. **Yield:** 8 servings.

Green Chili Corn Bread
Prep/Total Time: 30 min.

   1 package (8-1/2 ounces) corn bread/muffin mix
   1 egg
   2 tablespoons butter, melted
   1 can (11 ounces) Mexicorn, drained
   1 can (4 ounces) chopped green chilies, drained
1-1/2 cups (6 ounces) shredded pepper Jack cheese
 1/4 teaspoon hot pepper sauce

HONEY BUTTER:
 1/2 cup butter, softened
   2 tablespoons honey

In a large bowl, combine corn bread mix, egg and butter. Stir in the corn, chilies, cheese and hot pepper sauce.

Pour into a greased 11-in. x 7-in. x 2-in. baking dish. Bake at 400° for 20-22 minutes or until a toothpick comes out clean.

In a small bowl, combine butter and honey. Serve with warm bread. **Yield:** 8 servings.

Rocky Road Pudding
Prep: 15 min. + chilling

1-1/2 cups cold milk
   1 package (3.9 ounces) instant chocolate pudding mix
   1 carton (8 ounces) frozen whipped topping, thawed
   1 cup (6 ounces) semisweet chocolate chips
   1 cup miniature marshmallows, *divided*
 1/2 cup salted peanuts
 1/4 cup chocolate syrup, optional

In a large mixing bowl, beat milk and pudding mix on low speed for 2 minutes. Fold in the whipped topping, chocolate chips, 3/4 cup marshmallows and peanuts.

Pour into dessert dishes. Cover and refrigerate until set.

Just before serving, sprinkle with remaining marshmallows; drizzle with chocolate syrup if desired. **Yield:** 8 servings.

CUT YOUR TIME IN THE KITCHEN WITH THE SATISFYING FLAVOR OF FAMILY-PLEASING PORK

It was nearly an accident that Kenna Robinson came up with this half-hour meal. "I created the main dish by substituting pork for veal one night because that's what I had on hand," she explains from Sault Ste. Marie, Ontario. "Now, we have it twice per month.

"There is a similar story behind the salad. I started preparing a Caesar salad, but I ran out of ingredients. Luckily, my family loved the result, and now we have this version often.

"The mother of my shortcake recipe was necessity," Kenna adds. "I needed a quick way to use the berries we picked on a camping trip, and this yummy treat was the answer."

Pork Parmesan
Prep/Total Time: 25 min.

    1/2 cup dry bread crumbs
    1/4 cup grated Parmesan cheese
    1/4 teaspoon salt
    1/8 teaspoon pepper
    1/8 teaspoon paprika
      1 egg
      6 boneless pork loin chops (4 ounces *each*)
      2 tablespoons vegetable oil
    1/2 cup tomato sauce
      6 slices part-skim mozzarella cheese

In a shallow bowl, combine the bread crumbs, Parmesan cheese, salt, pepper and paprika. In another bowl, beat egg. Dip each pork chop in egg, then coat with crumb mixture.

In a large skillet, cook pork chops in oil over medium heat for 6 minutes on each side or until juices run clear. Top each chop with tomato sauce and cheese; cover and simmer for 1 minute or until cheese is melted. **Yield:** 6 servings.

Family Favorite Salad
Prep/Total Time: 10 min.

    1/4 cup vegetable oil
      1 garlic clove, minced
    1/4 teaspoon salt
    1/8 teaspoon pepper
      1 medium bunch romaine, torn
    1/2 cup chopped cucumber
    1/2 cup sliced celery
      2 tablespoons grated Parmesan cheese
      1 cup seasoned croutons

In a jar with tight-fitting lid, combine oil, garlic, salt and pepper; shake well and set aside. In a large bowl, combine remaining ingredients. Just before serving, shake dressing. Drizzle over salad; toss to coat. **Yield:** 6 servings.

Shortcake Supreme
Prep/Total Time: 10 min.

    2-1/4 cups fresh *or* frozen blueberries *and/or*
           raspberries, thawed
        2 to 3 tablespoons sugar
        1 envelope whipped topping mix
       12 thin slices angel food cake

In a large bowl, combine berries and sugar; set aside. Prepare the whipped topping mix according to package directions. Top cake slices with berries and whipped topping. **Yield:** 6 servings.

Quick TIP To prepare Pork Parmesan in a microwave, place breaded pork chops on a microwave-safe plate. (Omit the oil from the recipe.) Microwave on high for 4 minutes. Rotate plate and microwave 4 minutes longer or until pork juices run clear. Top with the tomato sauce and the cheese; microwave for 1-2 minutes or until the cheese is melted.

A HEARTWARMING MEAL IN MINUTES

Lemon Chicken

Prep/Total Time: 25 min.

Lori Schlecht • Wimbledon, North Dakota
I originally tried this recipe because I love the combination of rice and chicken. I made a few changes to suit my tastes and was pleased with how it looks and the short time needed to prepare it. Best of all, it is full of flavor and makes for a very comforting supper.

- 1 pound boneless skinless chicken breasts, cut into strips
- 1 medium onion, chopped
- 1 large carrot, thinly sliced
- 1 garlic clove, minced
- 2 tablespoons butter
- 1 tablespoon cornstarch
- 1 can (14-1/2 ounces) chicken broth
- 2 to 3 tablespoons fresh lemon juice
- 1 teaspoon grated lemon peel
- 1/2 teaspoon salt
- 1-1/2 cups uncooked instant rice
- 1 cup frozen chopped broccoli, thawed
- 1/4 cup minced fresh parsley

In a large skillet, cook chicken, onion, carrot and garlic in butter for about 5 minutes or until chicken is lightly browned and meat juices run clear; stirring occasionally.

In a large bowl, combine the cornstarch and broth; stir in lemon juice, peel, salt and rice. Add to skillet. Bring to a boil; cook and stir for 2 minutes or until thickened. Reduce heat; add broccoli and parsley. Cover and simmer 5-10 minutes or until rice is tender. **Yield:** 4 servings.

Quick Fruit Salad

Prep/Total Time: 10 min.

Sue Call • Beech Grove, Indiana
Here's a great way to round out any meal! Perfect for summer menus, Quick Fruit Salad is beautiful and refreshing as either a side dish or even for dessert. Try it with the canned pie filling of your choice, or switch out the fruit with whatever your gang enjoys most.

- 1 can (21 ounces) peach pie filling
- 3 firm bananas, sliced
- 2 cups strawberries, halved
- 1 cup seedless grapes

In a large salad bowl, combine all the ingredients. Refrigerate until serving. **Yield:** 6-8 servings.

Herb Bread

Prep/Total Time: 30 min.

Debbie Carlson • San Diego, California
This bread is an especially nice addition to last-minute meals. I'm so happy my mother shared the recipe because it's one my family asks for often. It's an easy way to turn bakery-bought bread into something special. Consider it the next time you need to complete a dinner, particularly if you're preparing Italian fare.

- 6 tablespoons butter, softened
- 1 to 2 garlic cloves, minced
- 2 teaspoons dried parsley flakes
- 1/2 teaspoon dried oregano
- 1/2 teaspoon dill weed
- 1 teaspoon grated Parmesan cheese
- 1 loaf sourdough *or* French bread, sliced

In a large bowl, combine the first six ingredients. Spread on one side of each bread slice; wrap loaf in foil. Bake at 350° for 20-25 minutes or until heated through. **Yield:** 6-8 servings.

Raspberry Breeze Pie (p. 98)

Desserts In a Dash

There's always room—and time—for dessert! Simply whip up any of the after-dinner delights featured here. Each of the no-stress specialties is guaranteed to satisfy the sweet tooth with only an ounce of effort.

Walnut Brownies

Raspberry Breeze Pie
(Pictured on page 96)
Prep/Total Time: 20 min.

Pamela Baldwin • Columbia, Tennessee
One way to my family's heart is through great-tasting food. Luckily, I've learned to take a few shortcuts to get there. Using canned pie filling and a prepared crust helps me put this tasty pie together in moments.

> 1 package (8 ounces) cream cheese, softened
> 1 cup confectioners' sugar
> 1 teaspoon vanilla extract
> 1 cup whipped topping
> 1 graham cracker crust (8 *or* 9 inches)
> 1-3/4 cups raspberry, cherry *or* strawberry pie filling
> 1/4 teaspoon almond extract
> Sliced almonds

In a large mixing bowl, beat the cream cheese, sugar and vanilla until smooth. Fold in the whipped topping. Spoon into crust. Combine the pie filling and extract; spread over the cream cheese layer. Garnish with sliced almonds. Chill until set. **Yield:** 6-8 servings.

Walnut Brownies
(Pictured above)
Prep/Total Time: 30 min.

Lorraine Silver • Chicopee, Massachusetts
I learned to make these quick brownies in a 1957 home economics class. They were the first goodies I'd ever baked by myself. Fifty years later, I still make them. The recipe calls for basic ingredients on hand in most every kitchen, and the rich chocolate flavor is delicious.

> 1/4 cup shortening
> 3 tablespoons baking cocoa
> 1 egg
> 1/2 cup sugar
> 1/4 teaspoon vanilla extract
> 1/2 cup all-purpose flour
> 1/4 teaspoon baking powder
> 1/8 teaspoon salt
> 1/4 cup chopped walnuts

In a small mixing bowl, cream shortening and cocoa; beat in egg, sugar and vanilla. Combine dry ingredients; gradually add to creamed mixture. Beat on low speed until thoroughly combined. Stir in walnuts.

Pour into a greased 8-in. x 4-in. x 2-in. loaf pan. Bake at 350° for 15-20 minutes or until a toothpick inserted near the center comes out clean. **Yield:** 8 brownies.

Banana Fritters
Prep/Total Time: 15 min.

Sharon Yonts • Scottsboro, Alabama
Scoops of vanilla ice cream are the perfect complement to these pieces of fried bananas. Try them yourself and you'll see what a delicious change they are from traditional ice cream toppings.

> 1 egg
> 1/3 cup milk
> 1 cup all-purpose flour
> 3 tablespoons sugar
> 1-1/2 teaspoons baking powder
> 1/4 teaspoon salt
> 6 medium firm bananas
> Oil for deep-fat frying
> Ice cream

In a large bowl, combine the first six ingredients. Cut the bananas in half lengthwise, then cut into 1-1/2-in. pieces. Coat bananas with egg mixture.

In an electric skillet, heat 1 in. of oil to 375°. Fry bananas for about 1 minute on each side or until golden brown. Drain on paper towels. Serve warm with ice cream. **Yield:** 6-8 servings.

Strawberry Cheesecake Trifle

(Pictured below)
Prep/Total Time: 20 min.

Lori Thorp • Frazee, Minnesota
The only drawback to this lovely dessert is that there's never any left over. For a patriotic look, replace one of the layers of strawberry pie filling with blueberry...or use whatever filling you prefer.

> 1 package (8 ounces) cream cheese, softened
> 1 cup (8 ounces) sour cream
> 1/2 cup cold milk
> 1 package (3.4 ounces) instant vanilla pudding mix
> 1 carton (12 ounces) frozen whipped topping, thawed
> 1-1/2 cups crushed butter-flavored crackers (about 38 crackers)
> 1/4 cup butter, melted
> 2 cans (21 ounces *each*) strawberry pie filling

In a large mixing bowl, beat the cream cheese until smooth. Beat in the sour cream; mix well.

In a small mixing bowl, beat milk and pudding mix on low speed for 2 minutes. Stir into cream cheese mixture. Fold in whipped topping.

In a small bowl, combine crackers and butter.

In a 2-1/2-qt. trifle bowl, layer half of the cream cheese mixture, crumbs and pie filling. Repeat layers. Refrigerate until serving. **Yield:** 12-16 servings.

Strawberry Cheesecake Trifle

County Fair Funnel Cakes

County Fair Funnel Cakes

(Pictured above)
Prep/Total Time: 30 min.

Our Test Kitchen staff happily whipped up these delicious, deep-fried pastries. To make the timeless treats, slowly swirl the batter into the oil, brown it to perfection and lightly dust with confectioners' sugar.

> 2 eggs, lightly beaten
> 1-1/2 cups milk
> 1/4 cup packed brown sugar
> 2 cups all-purpose flour
> 1-1/2 teaspoons baking powder
> 1/4 teaspoon salt
> Oil for deep-fat frying
> Confectioners' sugar

In a large bowl, combine the eggs, milk and brown sugar. Combine flour, baking powder and salt; beat into egg mixture until smooth. In an electric skillet or deep-fat fryer, heat oil to 375°. Cover the bottom of a funnel spout with your finger; ladle 1/2 cup batter into funnel. Holding the funnel several inches above the skillet release finger and move the funnel in a spiral motion until all of the batter is released (scraping funnel with a rubber spatula if needed).

Fry for 2 minutes on each side or until golden brown. Drain on paper towels. Repeat with remaining batter. Dust with confectioners' sugar; serve warm. **Yield:** 6 servings.

Pineapple Orange Cheesecake

Pineapple Orange Cheesecake
(Pictured above)
Prep/Total Time: 20 min.

A citrus topping jazzes up store-bought cheesecake in this idea from our Test Kitchen. It's the perfect way to add homespun flair to dessert time.

  2 cups cubed fresh pineapple
  2 tablespoons brown sugar
  2 tablespoons butter
1/3 cup orange marmalade
  1 package (30 ounces) frozen New York-style cheesecake, thawed
Whipped topping, optional

In a large skillet, saute pineapple and brown sugar in butter for 8 minutes. Spread orange marmalade over cheesecake; top with pineapple mixture. Garnish with the whipped topping if desired. **Yield:** 6 servings.

Mini Apple Pies
Prep/Total Time: 30 min.

Marsha Dingbaum • Aurora, California
A tube of refrigerated biscuits is the secret to these adorable, little treats. Loaded with down-home appeal, they're sure to become a favorite with your gang.

  1 tube (7-1/2 ounces) refrigerated biscuits
  1 tart apple, peeled and finely chopped
1/4 cup raisins
  3 tablespoons sugar
  1 teaspoon ground cinnamon
  2 tablespoons butter

Using a rolling pin, flatten each biscuit to a 3-in. to 4-in. circle. Combine the apple, raisins, sugar and

cinnamon; place a tablespoonful on each biscuit. Dot with butter. Bring up sides of biscuit to enclose filling and pinch to seal.

Place the pies in ungreased muffin cups. Bake at 375° for 11 to 13 minutes or until golden brown. **Yield:** 10 servings.

Chocolate Coconut Bars
(Pictured below)
Prep/Total Time: 30 min.

Carolyn Kyzer • Alexander, Arkansas
I think that it's impossible to resist this scrumptious dessert. With nuts, chocolate and a creamy cheesecake-like layer, these goodies taste like homemade candy bars. I keep the ingredients on hand so I can whip up a batch anytime.

  1 tube (8 ounces) refrigerated crescent rolls
  1 package (8 ounces) cream cheese, softened
1/3 cup confectioners' sugar
  1 egg
3/4 cup flaked coconut
  1 cup (6 ounces) semisweet chocolate chips
1/4 cup chopped nuts

Unroll crescent roll dough into one long rectangle on an ungreased baking sheet; seal seams and perforations. Roll out into a 13-in. x 9-in. rectangle, building up dough around edges.

In a small mixing bowl, beat the cream cheese, confectioners' sugar and egg until smooth; stir in coconut. Spread over crust.

Bake at 375° for 10-15 minutes or until cream cheese mixture is set. Immediately sprinkle with chips. Let stand for 5 minutes; spread melted chips over the top. Sprinkle with nuts. Cool completely before cutting. **Yield:** 2-1/2 dozen.

Chocolate Coconut Bars

Pistachio Dream Cake
Prep/Total Time: 30 min.

Audrey Grimm • Mesa, Arizona
A cake mix hurries along preparation of this frosted delight. Adding yogurt, pudding mix and a little lemon-lime soda to the batter makes the final product a true taste sensation.

- 1 package (18-1/4 ounces) yellow cake mix
- 1 package (1 ounce) instant sugar-free pistachio pudding mix
- 1 carton (8 ounces) nonfat plain yogurt
- 3 egg whites
- 1 teaspoon vanilla extract
- 1 cup diet lemon-lime soda

FROSTING:
- 1-1/2 cups cold skim milk
- 1 package (1 ounce) instant sugar-free pistachio pudding mix
- 2 cups reduced-fat whipped topping

In a large mixing bowl, combine dry cake and pudding mixes, yogurt, egg whites and vanilla; beat on low speed for 1 minute. Gradually beat in soda.

Pour into a 13-in. x 9-in. x 2-in. baking pan coated with nonstick cooking spray. Bake at 350° for 20-25 minutes or until a toothpick inserted near the center comes out clean. Cool.

For frosting, combine milk and dry pudding mix in a mixing bowl; beat on low for 2 minutes. Fold in whipped topping. Spread over cake. Store in the refrigerator. **Yield:** 20 servings.

Pineapple Fluff Pie
Prep/Total Time: 10 min.

Jane Rhodes • Silverdale, Washington
Thanks to convenience items such as canned pineapple and a prepared crust, 10 minutes are all you need to prepare this cool and refreshing no-bake dessert.

- 1 can (20 ounces) unsweetened crushed pineapple, drained
- 1 package (3.4 ounces) instant lemon pudding mix
- 1 carton (8 ounces) frozen whipped topping, thawed
- 1 graham cracker crust (9 inches)

In a large bowl, combine the pineapple and pudding mix until thickened; fold in the whipped topping. Spoon into crust. Refrigerate until serving. **Yield:** 8 servings.

Cool Raspberry Peach Pie

Cool Raspberry Peach Pie
(Pictured above)
Prep/Total Time: 30 min.

Mindee Myers • Lincoln, Nebraska
This pretty pie combines two of my favorite fruits. It makes the most of raspberries and peaches, and it's best during summer when the fruits are at their peak.

- 1-1/2 cups reduced-fat vanilla wafer crumbs (about 50 wafers)
- 2 tablespoons sugar
- 2 tablespoons butter
- 1 egg white

FILLING:
- 1/2 cup sugar
- 3 tablespoons cornstarch
- 1/4 cup water
- 4 cups sliced peeled fresh peaches *or* frozen unsweetened peach slices, thawed (about 1-1/2 pounds)
- 3 cups fresh raspberries

In a food processor, combine the wafer crumbs, sugar and butter; pulse until blended. Add egg white; pulse until moistened.

Press mixture onto the bottom and up the sides of a 9-in. pie plate. Bake at 375° for 8-10 minutes or until lightly browned. Cool completely on a wire rack.

In a large saucepan, combine sugar and cornstarch. Stir in water until smooth. Add peaches; stir to coat. Bring to a boil; cook and stir for 2 minutes or until thickened. Remove from the heat; gently stir in raspberries. Spoon into prepared crust. Chill until set. Refrigerate leftovers. **Yield:** 8 servings.

Peanut Butter Brownie Pizza

(Pictured below)
Prep/Total Time: 30 min.

Karen Jagger • Columbia City, Indiana
I constantly had cravings for peanut butter while I was expecting our second child. This dessert pizza satisfied me, and using a brownie mix meant I could throw it together in moments.

>   1   package brownie mix (8-inch square pan size)
>   1   package (8 ounces) cream cheese, softened
>   1/3   cup peanut butter
>   1/4   cup sugar
>   3   large ripe bananas, cut into 1/4-inch slices
>   1/2   cup orange *or* lemon juice
>   1/4   cup chopped peanuts
>   2   squares (1 ounce *each*) semisweet chocolate
>   2   teaspoons butter

Prepare brownie batter according to package directions and spread into a greased 12-in. pizza pan.

Bake at 375° for 15-20 minutes or until a toothpick inserted near the center comes out clean. Cool completely on a wire rack.

Meanwhile, in a large mixing bowl, beat the cream cheese, peanut butter and sugar until smooth. Spread over cooled crust. Toss bananas with juice; drain well. Arrange bananas over cream cheese mixture. Sprinkle with peanuts.

In a microwave, melt chocolate and butter; stir until smooth. Drizzle over bananas. Refrigerate until serving. **Yield:** 12 servings.

Peanut Butter Brownie Pizza

Pumpkin Crunch Parfaits

Pumpkin Crunch Parfaits

(Pictured above)
Prep/Total Time: 15 min.

Lorraine Darocha • Berkshire, Massachusetts
Here's a fun dessert that your youngsters can help make. It's great for Halloween or even after Thanksgiving dinner.

>   3/4   cup cold milk
>   1   package (3.4 ounces) instant vanilla pudding mix
>   2   cups whipped topping
>   1   cup canned pumpkin
>   1/2   teaspoon pumpkin pie spice
>   1   cup chopped pecans
>   32   gingersnap cookies, crushed (about 1-1/2 cups)
> Additional whipped topping

In a large mixing bowl, beat milk and pudding mix on low speed for 2 minutes. Stir in the whipped topping, pumpkin and pumpkin pie spice; mix well. Fold in pecans.

Spoon half of the mixture into parfait glasses; top with half of the gingersnap crumbs. Repeat layers. Top with additional whipped topping. **Yield:** 6 servings.

Cinnamon Bread Pudding

Prep/Total Time: 30 min.

Emma Magielda • Amsterdam, New York
I've used this recipe for more than 10 years, and people still ask for my secret. It's a deliciously different treat.

- 12 slices cinnamon bread, crusts removed
- 3 squares (1 ounce *each*) semisweet chocolate
- 2 cups half-and-half cream
- 1 cup milk
- 4 eggs
- 3/4 cup sugar
- 1-1/2 teaspoons vanilla extract

Cut bread in half diagonally. Arrange half of the slices in a single layer, overlapping if necessary, in an ungreased shallow 2-qt. microwave-safe dish. Drizzle with half of the chocolate; top with remaining bread.

In a 1-qt. microwave-safe bowl, combine the cream and milk; microwave, uncovered, on high for 4-6 minutes or until hot but not boiling.

In a small bowl, beat eggs; add sugar. Add a small amount of cream mixture; mix well. Return all to the larger bowl; stir in vanilla. Pour over bread; drizzle with the remaining chocolate.

Cover and microwave at 50% powder for 14-15 minutes or until a knife inserted near the center comes out clean, rotating a half-turn one (mixture will puff up during cooking). Uncover and let stand for 5 minutes. Serve warm or cold. Refrigerate leftovers. **Yield:** 6-8 servings.

German Chocolate Sundaes

Prep/Total Time: 20 min.

DeEtta Rasmussen • Fort Madison, Iowa
This terrific topping is a real surprise over chocolate ice cream. It's fun and fancy at the same time and much cooler to make on hot days than a cake.

- 1/2 cup sugar
- 1/2 cup evaporated milk
- 1/4 cup butter, cubed
- 2 egg yolks, lightly beaten
- 2/3 cup flaked coconut
- 1/2 cup chopped pecans
- 1 teaspoon vanilla extract

Chocolate ice cream
Chocolate syrup, toasted coconut and additional chopped pecans, optional

In a heavy saucepan, combine the sugar, milk, butter and egg yolks. Bring to a boil over medium heat, stirring constantly; cook and stir for 2 minutes or until thickened.

Remove from the heat. Stir in the coconut, pecans and vanilla. Stir until the sauce is cooled slightly. Serve over ice cream. Top with the chocolate syrup, coconut and pecans if desired. **Yield:** 1-1/4 cups.

Berry Cheesecake Parfaits

(Pictured below)
Prep/Total Time: 10 min.

Joyce Mart • Wichita, Kansas
I can serve up this refreshing dessert in no time. Impressive and delightful, it seems to be just the right touch after a full meal. I also recommend it as a late-night snack.

- 1 package (8 ounces) cream cheese, softened
- 2 to 4 tablespoons sugar
- 1/2 cup vanilla yogurt
- 2 cups fresh raspberries *or* berries of your choice
- 1/2 cup graham cracker crumbs (8 squares)

In a large mixing bowl, beat cream cheese and sugar until smooth. Stir in yogurt. In 4 parfait glasses or bowls, alternate layers of berries, cream cheese mixture and cracker crumbs. Serve immediately or refrigerate for up to 8 hours. **Yield:** 4 servings.

Berry Cheesecake Parfaits

Fruit-Filled Angel Food Torte

Fruit-Filled Angel Food Torte
(Pictured above)
Prep/Total Time: 15 min.

Hettie Johnson • Jacksonville, Florida
Tired of eating plain angel food cake and fruit for dessert, I decided to combine the two with a little whipped topping—the result is this scrumptious and impressive torte. It tastes as good as it looks, and it comes together in less than a half hour.

    1 **carton (12 ounces) frozen whipped topping, thawed, *divided***
    1 **can (15 ounces) fruit cocktail, drained**
    1 **prepared angel food cake (10 inches)**
    1 **can (11 ounces) mandarin oranges, drained**
    1 **large navel orange, sliced, optional**
Fresh mint, optional

Fold 1-1/2 cups whipped topping into fruit cocktail just until blended. Split cake horizontally into three layers; place one layer on a serving plate. Spread with half of the fruit mixture. Repeat layers. Top with remaining cake layer.

Frost top and sides with remaining whipped topping. Arrange mandarin oranges on top. Refrigerate until serving. Serve with orange slices and mint if desired. **Yield:** 12 servings.

Whoopie Pies
Prep/Total Time: 25 min.

Ruth Ann Stelfox • Raymond, Alberta
These soft, moist little treats have been a favorite of mine for many years. They're a wonderful change from most cookies, brownies and other sweets. For a fun surprise, tuck one or two into the brown-bag lunch of a loved one.

    1 **cup butter, softened**
1-1/2 **cups sugar**
    2 **teaspoons vanilla extract**
    2 **eggs**
    4 **cups all-purpose flour**
3/4 **cup baking cocoa**
1/2 **teaspoon salt**
    2 **teaspoon baking soda**
    1 **cup water**
    1 **cup buttermilk**
FILLING:
    2 **cups marshmallow creme**
    2 **cups confectioners' sugar**
1/2 **cup butter, softened**
    2 **teaspoons vanilla extract**

In a large mixing bowl, beat butter, sugar, vanilla and eggs until creamy. Combine dry ingredients; add to butter mixture alternately with water and buttermilk.

Drop by teaspoonfuls onto greased baking sheets. Bake at 375° for 5-7 minutes or until done. Cool completely.

In a small mixing bowl, beat filling ingredients until fluffy. Spread filling on half of the cookies, then top with remaining cookies. **Yield:** 18 cookies.

Simple Lime Mousse
Prep/Total Time: 10 min.

Shirley Glaab • Hattiesburg, Mississippi
Here's a light mousse that's perfect after a heavy, full-flavored meal. It's an ideal pairing of zesty lime and fluffy whipped cream.

    1 **cup heavy whipping cream**
1/4 **cup sugar**
    2 **tablespoons lime juice**
    1 **tablespoon grated lime peel**
    1 **teaspoon vanilla extract**
Lime slices and fresh mint, optional

In a mixing bowl, combine the cream, sugar, lime juice, peel and vanilla. Beat on high speed until soft peaks form, about 4 minutes. Spoon into dessert dishes. Garnish with lime slices and mint if desired. **Yield:** 4 servings.

Super Chunky Cookies

(Pictured below)
Prep/Total Time: 30 min.

Rebecca Jendry • Spring Branch, Texas
Chocolate lovers will go crazy over these cookies that feature three kinds of chocolate! When friends ask me to make "those cookies," I know exactly what recipe they are talking about.

  1/2 cup butter-flavored shortening
  1/2 cup butter, softened
    1 cup packed brown sugar
  3/4 cup sugar
    2 eggs
    2 teaspoons vanilla extract
2-1/2 cups all-purpose flour
    1 teaspoon baking soda
  1/8 teaspoon salt
    1 cup miniature semisweet chocolate chips
    1 cup milk chocolate chips
    1 cup vanilla *or* white chips
    4 squares (1 ounces *each*) bittersweet
      chocolate, coarsely chopped
  3/4 cup English toffee bits *or* almond brickle
      chips
  1/2 cup chopped pecans

In a mixing bowl, cream shortening, butter and sugars. Add eggs, one at a time, beating well after each addition. Beat in vanilla. Combine flour, baking soda and salt; gradually add to the creamed mixture. Stir in the remaining ingredients.

Drop by tablespoonfuls 3 in. apart on ungreased baking sheets. Bake at 350° for 10-12 minutes or until lightly browned. Cool for 2-3 minutes before removing the cookies to wire racks to cool completely. **Yield:** 8-1/2 dozen.

Super Chunky Cookies

Chocolate Mallow Pie

Chocolate Mallow Pie

(Pictured above)
Prep/Total Time: 20 min.

Glenda Parsonage • Maple Creek, Saskatchewan
Five items are all you need for this after-dinner delight. Light and fluffy, it's a no-fuss sensation that you'll turn to time and again.

    1 package (8 ounces) cream cheese, softened
    2 cups cold milk, *divided*
    1 package (3.9 ounces) instant chocolate
      pudding mix
1-1/2 cups miniature marshmallows
    1 graham cracker crust (9 inches)

In a large mixing bowl, beat cream cheese and 1/2 cup milk until smooth. Add pudding mix and remaining milk; mix well. Fold in the marshmallows. Pour into the crust. Refrigerate until serving. **Yield:** 6-8 servings.

Quick TIP

For easy cleanup, purchase a roll of parchment paper. Available at most grocery stores, the paper is ideal for lining pans when baking cookies. By simply discarding the paper between each batch and replacing it with a new sheet, you'll avoid having to wash the pan time after time.

Index

General Recipe Index

✤ **Recipe is ready in 15 minutes or less.**

❖ **Recipe is ready in 15 minutes or less.**

✤ **Recipe is ready in 15 minutes or less.**

✤ **Recipe is ready in 15 minutes or less.**

✤ **Recipe is ready in 15 minutes or less.**

Index

Alphabetical Index

✤ **Recipe is ready in 15 minutes or less.**

✤ **Recipe is ready in 15 minutes or less.**